WHAT'S COOKING
vegetarian

Jenny Stacey

THUNDER BAY
P·R·E·S·S

First published in the United States in 1999 by
Thunder Bay Press
An imprint of the Advantage Publishers Group
5880 Oberlin Drive
San Diego, CA 92121-4794
www.advantagebooksonline.com

Library of Congress Cataloging in Publication Data.

Stacey, Jenny
     What's cooking , Vegetarian/Jenny Stacey
          p.   cm.
     ISBN 1-57145-181-1
     1. Vegetarian cookery   I. Title   II. Title Vegetarian
TX837.S72   1999
641.5'636--dc21
                                                            98-86390
                                                            CIP

Printed in China

3 4 5 00 01 02

Produced by Haldane Mason, London

Acknowledgments
Art Director: Ron Samuels
Editorial Director: Sydney Francis
Managing Editor: Jo-Anne Cox
Editorial Assistant: Elizabeth Towers
Design: dap ltd
Photography: St John Asprey
Home Economist: Jacqueline Bellefontaine
North American Managing Editor: JoAnn Padgett
North American Project Editor: Elizabeth McNulty

The publishers would like to thank the british Chicken Information Service for pro-
Viding the recipes on pages 14-17,38-41,44,48,52,58,64,70-75,78-83,88-93,
96-101,104,112,116,122,130,134,138,142,148,152-159,162,166,170,174-181,
184-187,192-225,228-233,236-241,244,248-255

Note

Unless otherwise stated, milk is assumed to be full fat, eggs are medium,
and pepper is freshly ground black pepper.
Front cover: Broiled Chicken with Pesto Toasts (pages 208-209)
Back cover: Sticky Chicken Drumsticks with Mango Salsa (pages 40-41)

Contents

Introduction

This book is designed to appeal to vegetarians, demi-vegetarians, and vegans alike. Its main aim is to dispel the myth that vegetarian food is brown, stodgy, and bland. When browsing through the recipes in this cookbook, you will discover just how versatile, colorful, and flavorful a vegetarian diet can be.

It makes perfect sense when you consider the wide range of natural produce that is generally available year round. With the advent of refrigerated transportation, fresh produce is now brought from all over the world to give us a whole array of fresh fruit and vegetables with which to work. In addition, the use of spices, fresh herbs, and garlic, accompanied by sauces and relishes makes for a very exciting and healthy diet.

Eating a balanced, nutritional diet is very important and can be easily achieved by combining the recipes in this book, when planning your meal, to include protein, carbohydrate, vitamins, minerals, and some fats. It is very important in any diet, but especially a vegetarian diet, that a good balance is achieved and that sufficient protein is eaten.

The recipes in this book come from far and wide, including China and Asia, the Middle East, and the Mediterranean. There are also more traditional recipes and variations on themes, such as "vegetable-toad-in-the-hole", a quick, tasty family meal in which it is guaranteed you won't miss the meat. Indeed, this can be said for all of the recipes in this book. Many could be served to meat-eating guests without them missing the "meat factor" in any way. In fact, this book is the perfect way to introduce your friends to this healthy and delicious diet.

When cooking the following recipes, feel free to substitute some ingredients to suit your specific diets, using soy milk for example in place of cow's milk, cream substitute instead of dairy cream, and vegetable margarine in place of butter. You will discover that the vegetarian diet has progressed greatly from the nut cutlet to a colorful and imaginative way of eating. Go ahead and enjoy!

THE VEGETARIAN CUPBOARD

A well-stocked cupboard forms the backbone of any good cook's kitchen, and it is always useful to have plenty of basic foods at hand. Use the following information as a checklist when you need to replenish your stocks.

Flour

You will need to keep a selection of different kinds of flour: all-purpose and self-rising flour if you want to make your own bread, and whole wheat flour, either for using on its own or for combining with white flour for cakes and pastries. You may also like to keep some rice flour and cornstarch for thickening sauces and to add to cakes, cookies, and puddings. Buckwheat, garbanzo bean, and soy flours can also be bought. These are useful for pancakes and for combining with other flours to add different flavors and textures.

Grains

A good variety of grains is essential. For rice, choose from long-grain, basmati, Italian arborio for making risotto, short-grain for puddings, and wild rice to add interest. Look out for fragrant Thai rice, jasmine rice, and combinations of different varieties to add color and texture to your dishes. When choosing your rice, remember that brown rice is a better source of vitamin B1 and fiber.

Other grains add variety to the diet. Try to include some barley (whole grain or pearl), millet, bulgur wheat, polenta (made from corn), oats (oatmeal, oat flakes, or oat bran), semolina—including cous-cous (from which it is made), sago, and tapioca.

Pasta

Pasta is so popular nowadays, and there are many types and shapes to choose from. Keep a good selection, and always make sure you have the basic lasagne sheets, tagliatelle or fettuccine (flat ribbons), and spaghetti. Try spinach- or tomato-flavored varieties for a change, and sample some of the many fresh pastas now available. Better still, make your own—hand rolling pasta, while undoubtedly time-consuming, can be very satisfying, but you can buy a special machine for rolling the dough and cutting certain shapes. You could also buy a wooden "pasta tree" on which to hang the pasta to dry, in which case you might find you get enthusiastic help especially if you have small children!

Legumes

Legumes, also called pulses, are a valuable source of protein, vitamins, and minerals. Stock up on soy beans, navy beans, red kidney beans, cannellini beans, garbanzo beans, lentils, split peas, and dried lima beans. Buy dried legumes for soaking and cooking yourself, or canned varieties for speed and convenience. Cook dried red and black kidney beans in boiling water for 15 minutes to destroy harmful toxins in the outer skin. Drain and rinse the beans, and then simmer until the beans are tender. Soy beans should be boiled for 1 hour, as they contain a substance that inhibits protein absorption.

Spices and herbs

A good selection of spices and herbs is important for adding variety and interest to your cooking. There are some good spice mixtures available—try Cajun, Chinese five-spice, Indonesian piri-piri, and the different curry blends. Try grinding your own spices with a mortar and pestle or in a coffee mill to make your own blends, or just experiment with those that you can buy. Although spices will keep well, don't leave them in the cupboard for too long, as they may lose some of their strength. Buy small amounts as you need them.

Fresh herbs are preferable to dried, but it is essential to have dried ones in stock as a useful back-up. Keep the basics such as thyme, rosemary, and bay leaves.

Chilies

These come both fresh and dried and in colors from green through yellow, orange and red to brown. The "hotness" varies so use with caution, but as a guide the smaller they are the hotter they will be. The seeds are hottest and are usually discarded. When cutting chilies with bare hands do not touch your eyes; the juices will cause severe irritation.

Chili powder should also be used sparingly. Check whether the powder is pure chili or a chili seasoning or blend, which should be milder. Chili sauces are also used widely in Asian cookery, but again they vary in strength from hot to exceedingly hot, as well as in sweetness.

Nuts and seeds

As well as adding protein, vitamins, and useful fats to the diet, nuts and seeds add important flavor and texture to vegetarian meals. To bring out the flavor of nuts and seeds, broil or dry-fry them until lightly browned.

Make sure that you keep a good supply of almonds, Brazils, cashews, chestnuts (dried or canned), hazelnuts, peanuts, pecans, pistachios, pine nuts, and walnuts. Coconut—either creamed or shredded—is useful too.

For your seed collection, have sesame, sunflower, pumpkin, and poppy. Pumpkin seeds in particular are a good source of zinc.

Dried fruits

Currants, raisins, golden raisins, dates, apples, apricots, figs, pears, peaches, prunes, papayas, mangoes, figs, bananas, and pineapples can all be purchased dried and can be used in lots of different recipes. When buying dried fruits, look for untreated varieties: for example, buy figs that have not been rolled in sugar, and choose unsulfured apricots, if they are available.

Oils and fats

Oils are useful for adding subtle flavorings to foods, so it is a good idea to have a selection in your cupboard. Use a light olive oil for cooking and extra-virgin olive oil for salad dressings. Use sunflower oil as a good general-purpose oil and select one or two specialty oils to add character to different dishes. Sesame oil is wonderful in stir-fries; hazelnut and walnut oils are superb in salad dressings. Oils and fats add flavor to foods, and contain the important fat-soluble vitamins A, D, E, and K. Remember all fats and oils are high in calories, and that oils are higher in calories than butter or margarine—1 tbsp. of oil contains 134 calories, whereas 1 tbsp. of butter or margarine contains 110 calories. When you are using oil, it is a good idea to measure it—it is easy to use twice as much without realizing it.

Vinegars

Choose three or four vinegars—red or white wine, apple, light malt, tarragon, sherry, or balsamic vinegar, to name just a few. Each will add its own character to your recipes.

Mustards

Mustards are made from black, brown, or white mustard seeds, which are ground, mixed with spices, and then, usually, mixed with vinegar. Meaux mustard is made from mixed mustard seeds and has a grainy texture with a warm, spicy taste. Dijon mustard, made from husked and ground mustard seeds, is medium-hot and has a sharp flavor. Its versatility in salads and with barbecues makes it ideal for the vegetarian. German mustard is mild sweet/sour and is best used in Scandinavian and German dishes.

Bottled sauces

Soy sauce is widely used in Chinese and Southeast Asian cookery and is made from fermented yellow soy beans mixed with wheat, salt, yeast, and sugar. Light soy sauce tends to be rather salty, whereas dark soy sauce tends to be sweeter and is more often used in dips and sauces. Teriyaki sauce gives an authentic Japanese flavoring to stir-fries. Thick and dark brown, it contains soy sauce, vinegar, sesame oil, and spices as main ingredients. Black bean and yellow bean sauces add an instant authentic Chinese flavor to stir-fries. Black bean sauce is the stronger; the yellow bean variety is milder and is excellent with vegetables.

Soups & Starters

Soup is simple to make, but always produces tasty results. There is an enormous variety of soups that you can make with vegetables. They can be rich and creamy, thick and chunky, light and delicate, and hot or chilled. The vegetables are often puréed to give a smooth consistency and thicken the soup, but you can also purée just some of the mixture to give the soup more texture and interest. A wide range of ingredients can be used in addition to vegetables—legumes, grains, noodles, cheese, and yogurt are all good candidates. It is also easy to make substitutions when you do not have certain ingredients at hand.

Starters are an important part of any meal, setting the scene for the remainder of the menu and whetting the appetite. They should therefore be colorful and full of flavor, but balance the remainder of the meal well, not being too filling if a heavier main course is being served, or containing ingredients used in following courses.

With this in mind, this chapter is packed with a range of thick and thin flavorful soups for all occasions and a wide range of starters from different origins, be it Chinese, Souteast Asian, Indian, or Mediterranean, they will all make a wonderful start to a meal.

Mixed Bean Soup

This is a really hearty soup, filled with color, flavor, and goodness,
which may be adapted to any vegetables that you have at hand.

Serves 4

INGREDIENTS

1 tablespoon vegetable oil
1 red onion, halved and sliced
²/₃ cup diced potato
1 carrot, diced
1 leek, sliced
1 green chili, sliced
3 garlic cloves, crushed

1 teaspoon ground coriander
1 teaspoon chili powder
4 cups vegetable stock
1 pound mixed canned beans,
   such as red kidney, borlotti,
   or flageolet, drained
salt and pepper

2 tablespoons chopped cilantro,
   to garnish

1 Heat the vegetable oil in a large saucepan and add the prepared onion, potato, carrot, and leek. Sauté for about 2 minutes, stirring, until the vegetables are slightly softened.

2 Add the sliced chili and crushed garlic and cook for a further 1 minute.

3 Stir in the ground coriander, chili powder, and the vegetable stock.

4 Bring the soup to a boil, reduce the heat, and cook for 20 minutes, or until the vegetables are tender.

5 Stir in the beans, season to taste with salt and pepper, and cook for a further 10 minutes, stirring occasionally.

6 Transfer the soup to a warm tureen or individual bowls, garnish with chopped cilantro, and serve at once.

COOK'S TIP

Serve this soup with slices of warm corn bread or a cheese loaf.

Vegetable & Corn Chowder

This is a really filling soup, which should be served before a lighter meal.
Packed with corn and fresh vegetables, it is easy to prepare and filled with flavor.

Serves 4

INGREDIENTS

1 tablespoon vegetable oil
1 red onion, diced
1 red bell pepper, diced
3 garlic cloves, crushed
1 large potato, diced
2 tablespoons all-purpose flour

$2^1/_2$ cups milk
$1^1/_4$ cups vegetable stock
$1^3/_4$ oz broccoli florets
3 cups canned corn, drained
$^3/_4$ cup grated vegetarian
    Cheddar cheese

salt and pepper
1 tablespoon chopped fresh cilantro,
    to garnish

1 Heat the oil in a large saucepan and sauté the onion, bell pepper, garlic, and potato for 2–3 minutes, stirring.

2 Stir in the flour and cook for 30 seconds. Stir in the milk and stock.

3 Add the broccoli florets and corn. Bring the mixture to a boil, stirring, then reduce the heat and simmer for about 20 minutes, or until the vegetables are tender.

4 Stir in ½ cup of the grated cheese until it melts.

5 Season and spoon the chowder into a warm soup tureen. Garnish with the remaining cheese and the cilantro and serve.

COOK'S TIP

Add a little heavy cream to the soup after adding the milk for a really creamy flavor.

COOK'S TIP

Vegetarian cheeses are made with rennets of nonanimal origin, using microbial or fungal enzymes.

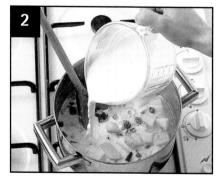

Cauliflower & Broccoli Soup with Swiss Cheese

Full of flavor, this creamy cauliflower and broccoli soup is simple to make and delicious to eat.

Serves 4

INGREDIENTS

3 tablespoons vegetable oil
1 red onion, chopped
2 garlic cloves, crushed
$10^{1}/_{2}$ oz cauliflower florets
$10^{1}/_{2}$ oz broccoli florets
1 tablespoon all-purpose flour

$2^{1}/_{2}$ cups milk
$1^{1}/_{4}$ cups vegetable stock
$^{3}/_{4}$ cup grated vegetarian Swiss cheese
pinch of paprika
$^{2}/_{3}$ cup light cream

paprika and vegetarian Swiss cheese shavings, to garnish

1 Heat the oil in a large saucepan and sauté the onion, garlic, cauliflower, and broccoli for 3–4 minutes, stirring constantly. Add the flour and cook for a further 1 minute, stirring.

2 Stir in the milk and stock and bring to a boil. Reduce the heat and simmer for 20 minutes.

3 Remove about a quarter of the vegetables and set aside.

4 Put the remaining soup in a food processor and process for 30 seconds, until smooth. Transfer the soup to a clean saucepan.

5 Return the reserved vegetable pieces to the soup.

6 Stir in the grated cheese, paprika, and light cream and heat gently for 2–3 minutes without boiling, or until the cheese starts to melt.

7 Transfer to warm soup bowls, garnish with shavings of Swiss cheese and dust with paprika.

COOK'S TIP

The soup must not start to boil after the cream has been added, otherwise it will curdle. Use unsweetened yogurt instead of the cream if desired, but again do not allow to boil.

Celery, Stilton, & Walnut Soup

This is a classic combination of ingredients all brought together in a delicious, creamy soup.

Serves 4

INGREDIENTS

4 tablespoons butter
2 shallots, chopped
3 celery stalks, chopped
1 garlic clove, crushed
2 tablespoons all-purpose flour

$2^{1}/_{2}$ cups vegetable stock
$1^{1}/_{4}$ cups milk
$1^{1}/_{2}$ cups crumbled blue Stilton cheese, plus extra to garnish
2 tablespoons walnut halves, roughly chopped

$^{2}/_{3}$ cup unsweetened yogurt
salt and pepper
chopped celery leaves, to garnish

1 Melt the butter in a large saucepan and sauté the shallots, celery, and garlic for 2–3 minutes, stirring constantly, until softened.

2 Add the all-purpose flour and cook, stirring constantly, for 30 seconds.

3 Gradually stir in the stock and milk and bring to a boil.

4 Reduce the heat to a gentle simmer and add the crumbled blue Stilton cheese and walnut halves. Cover and simmer for 20 minutes.

5 Stir in the unsweetened yogurt and heat for a further 2 minutes without boiling.

6 Season the soup to taste with salt and pepper, then transfer to a warm soup tureen or individual serving bowls, garnish with chopped celery leaves and extra crumbled blue Stilton cheese, and serve at once.

COOK'S TIP

As well as adding protein, vitamins, and useful fats to the diet, nuts add important flavor and texture to vegetarian meals.

VARIATION

Use an alternative blue cheese, such as Dolcelatte or Gorgonzola, if desired, or a strong vegetarian Cheddar cheese, grated.

Curried Parsnip Soup

Parsnips make a delicious soup, as they have a slightly sweet flavor. In this recipe,
spices are added to complement this sweetness and a dash of lemon juice adds tartness.

Serves 4

INGREDIENTS

1 tablespoon vegetable oil
1 tablespoon butter
1 red onion, chopped
3 parsnips, chopped
2 garlic cloves, crushed

2 teaspoon garam masala
$1/2$ teaspoon chili powder
1 tablespoon all-purpose flour
$3^3/4$ cups vegetable stock
grated rind and juice of 1 lemon

salt and pepper
lemon zest, to garnish

1 Heat the oil and butter in a large saucepan until the butter has melted.

2 Add the onion, parsnips, and garlic and sauté for 5–7 minutes, stirring, until the vegetables have softened.

3 Add the garam masala and chili powder and cook for 30 seconds, stirring well.

4 Sprinkle in the flour, mixing well and cook for a further 30 seconds.

5 Stir in the stock, lemon rind, and juice and bring to a boil. Reduce the heat and simmer for 20 minutes.

6 Remove some of the vegetable pieces with a slotted spoon and reserve until required. Process the remaining soup and vegetables in a food processor for 1 minute, or until smooth.

7 Return the soup to a clean saucepan and stir in the reserved vegetables. Heat the soup through for 2 minutes.

8 Season, then transfer to soup bowls, garnish with grated lemon zest, and serve.

VARIATION

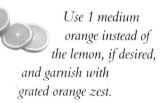

Use 1 medium orange instead of the lemon, if desired, and garnish with grated orange zest.

Jerusalem Artichoke Soup

Jerusalem artichokes belong to the tuber family. They are native to North America, but are now widely grown elsewhere. They have a delicious nutty flavor, which combines well with orange.

Serves 4

INGREDIENTS

1^1/$_2$ pounds Jerusalem artichokes
5 tablespoons orange juice
2 tablespoons butter
1 leek, chopped

1 garlic clove, crushed
1^1/$_4$ cups vegetable stock
^{2}/$_3$ cup milk
2 tablespoons chopped cilantro

^{2}/$_3$ cup unsweetened yogurt
grated orange rind, to garnish

1 Rinse the Jerusalem artichokes and place in a large saucepan with 2 tablespoons of the orange juice and enough water to cover. Bring to a boil, reduce the heat, and cook for 20 minutes, or until the artichokes are tender.

2 Drain the artichokes, reserving 2 cups of the cooking liquid. Set the artichokes aside to cool.

3 Once cooled, peel the artichokes and place in a large bowl. Mash the flesh with a potato masher.

4 Melt the butter in a large saucepan and sauté the leek and garlic, stirring, for about 2–3 minutes, until the leek softens.

5 Stir in the artichoke flesh, the reserved cooking water, the stock, milk, and remaining orange juice. Bring the soup to a boil, reduce the heat, and simmer for 2–3 minutes.

6 Remove a few pieces of leek with a slotted spoon and reserve. Transfer remaining soup to a food processor and process for 1 minute, until smooth.

7 Return the soup to a clean saucepan and stir in the reserved leeks, cilantro, and yogurt.

8 Transfer to individual soup bowls, garnish with orange rind, and serve.

VARIATION

If Jerusalem artichokes are unavailable, you could use sweet potatoes instead.

Red Bell Pepper & Chili Soup

This soup has a real Mediterranean flavor, using sweet red bell peppers, tomato, chili, and basil. It is great served with a warm olive bread.

Serves 4

INGREDIENTS

8 oz red bell peppers,
   seeded and sliced
1 onion, sliced
2 garlic cloves, crushed
1 green chili, chopped

$1^1/_2$ cups sieved tomatoes
$2^1/_2$ cups vegetable stock
2 tablespoons chopped basil
fresh basil sprigs, to garnish

1 Put the bell peppers in a large, heavy-based saucepan, together with the onion, garlic, and chili. Add the sieved tomatoes and vegetable stock and bring to a boil, stirring well.

2 Reduce the heat to a simmer and cook for 20 minutes, or until the bell peppers have softened. Drain, reserving the liquid and vegetables separately.

3 Press the vegetables through a strainer with the back of a wooden spoon. Alternatively, put them in a food processor and process until smooth.

4 Return the vegetable purée to a clean saucepan with the reserved cooking liquid. Add the basil and heat through until hot. Garnish the soup with fresh basil sprigs and serve.

COOK'S TIP

Basil is a useful herb to grow at home. It can be grown easily in a window box.

VARIATION

This soup is also delicious served chilled with $2/_3$ cup of unsweetened yogurt swirled into it.

Dhal Soup

*Dhal is the name given to a delicious Indian lentil dish. This soup is a variation of the theme—
it is made with red lentils and spiced with curry powder.*

Serves 4

INGREDIENTS

2 tablespoons butter
2 garlic cloves, crushed
1 onion, chopped
$^1/_2$ teaspoon turmeric
1 teaspoon garam masala
$^1/_4$ teaspoon chili powder
1 teaspoon ground cumin

2$^1/_4$ pounds canned, chopped
   tomatoes, drained
1 cup red lentils
2 teaspoons lemon juice
2$^1/_2$ cups vegetable stock

1$^1/_4$ cups coconut milk
salt and pepper
chopped cilantro and lemon slices,
   to garnish
nan bread, to serve

1 Melt the butter in a large saucepan and sauté the garlic and onion for 2–3 minutes, stirring. Add the spices and cook for a further 30 seconds.

2 Stir in the tomatoes, red lentils, lemon juice, vegetable stock, and coconut milk and bring to a boil.

3 Reduce the heat and simmer for 25–30 minutes, until the lentils are tender and cooked.

4 Season to taste and spoon the soup into a warm tureen. Garnish with cilantro and lemon and serve with warm nan bread.

COOK'S TIP

You can buy cans of coconut milk from supermarkets and specialty grocers. Coconut milk is also available in a lighter, reduced-fat version.

COOK'S TIP

Add small quantities of hot water to the pan while the lentils are cooking if they begin to absorb too much of the liquid.

Avocado & Vegetable Soup

Avocado has a rich flavor and color, which makes a creamy flavored soup.
It is best served chilled, but may be eaten warm as well.

Serves 4

INGREDIENTS

1 large, ripe avocado
2 tablespoons lemon juice
1 tablespoon vegetable oil
$1/2$ cup canned corn, drained
2 tomatoes, peeled and seeded
1 garlic clove, crushed

1 leek, chopped
1 red chili, chopped
2 cups vegetable stock
$2/3$ cup milk
shredded leeks, to garnish

1 Peel and mash the avocado with a fork, stir in the lemon juice, and reserve until required.

2 Heat the oil in a pan and sauté the corn, tomatoes, garlic, leek, and chili for about 2–3 minutes, or until the vegetables are softened.

3 Put half of the vegetable mixture in a food processor or blender with the avocado and process until smooth. Transfer to a clean saucepan.

4 Add the stock, milk, and reserved vegetables and cook gently for 3–4 minutes, until hot. Garnish and serve.

COOK'S TIP

To remove the pit from an avocado, first cut the avocado in half, then holding one half in your hand, rap the pit with a knife until it is embedded in the pit, then twist the knife until the pit is dislodged.

COOK'S TIP

If serving chilled, transfer from the food processor to a bowl, stir in the stock and milk, cover, and chill in the refrigerator for at least 4 hours.

Spanish Tomato Soup
with Garlic Bread Croûtons

This Mediterranean tomato soup is thickened with bread,
as is traditional in some parts of Spain.

Serves 4

INGREDIENTS

4 tablespoons olive oil
1 onion, chopped
3 garlic cloves, crushed
1 green bell pepper, chopped
1/2 teaspoon chili powder
1 pound tomatoes, chopped

8 oz French or
  Italian bread, cubed
4 cups vegetable stock

GARLIC BREAD:
4 slices French or Italian bread
4 tablespoons olive oil
2 garlic cloves, crushed
1/4 cup grated vegetarian
  Cheddar cheese
chili powder, to garnish

1 Heat the olive oil in a large skillet and add the prepared onion, garlic, and bell pepper. Sauté the vegetables for 2–3 minutes or until the onion is soft and translucent.

2 Add the chili powder and tomatoes and cook over medium heat until the mixture has thickened.

3 Stir in the bread cubes and stock and cook for about 10–15 minutes, until the soup is thick and fairly smooth.

4 To make the garlic bread, toast the bread slices under a preheated broiler. Drizzle the oil over the top of the bread, rub with the garlic, sprinkle with the grated cheese, and return to the broiler for 2–3 minutes, until the cheese has melted and is bubbling. Sprinkle with chili powder and serve at once with the soup.

VARIATION

Replace the green bell pepper
with red bell pepper,
if desired.

Fava Bean & Mint Soup

Fresh fava beans are best for this recipe, but if they are unavailable, use frozen beans instead. They combine well with the fresh flavor of mint.

Serves 4

INGREDIENTS

2 tablespoons olive oil

1 red onion, chopped

2 garlic cloves, crushed

2 potatoes, diced

3 cups fava beans,
   thawed if frozen

$3^3/_4$ cups vegetable stock

2 tablespoons freshly chopped mint

fresh mint sprigs and unsweetened
   yogurt, to garnish

1 Heat the olive oil in a large saucepan and sauté the onion and garlic for 2–3 minutes, until soft and translucent.

2 Add the potatoes and cook for 5 minutes, stirring well.

3 Stir in the beans and the stock, cover, and simmer for 30 minutes, or until the beans and potatoes are tender.

4 Remove a few vegetables with a slotted spoon and set aside until required. Place the remainder of the soup in a food processor or blender and process until smooth.

5 Return the soup to a clean saucepan and add the reserved vegetables and mint. Stir well and heat through gently.

6 Transfer the soup to a warm tureen or individual serving bowls. Garnish with swirls of yogurt and sprigs of fresh mint and serve immediately.

VARIATION

Use chopped fresh cilantro and ½ teaspoon ground cumin as flavorings in the soup, if desired.

Crispy Potato Skins

Potato skins are always a favorite. Prepare the skins in advance and warm through before serving with the salad fillings.

Serves 4

INGREDIENTS

4 large baking potatoes
2 tablespoons vegetable oil
4 teaspoons salt
snipped chives, to garnish
²/3 cup sour cream and 2 tablespoons
   chopped chives, to serve

BEAN SPROUT SALAD:
¹/2 cup bean sprouts
1 celery stalk, sliced
1 orange, peeled and segmented
1 red eating apple, chopped
¹/2 red bell pepper, chopped
1 tablespoon chopped parsley
1 tablespoon light soy sauce
1 tablespoon clear honey
1 small garlic clove, crushed

BEAN FILLING:
1¹/2 cups canned, mixed
   beans, drained
1 onion, halved and sliced
1 tomato, chopped
2 scallions, chopped
2 teaspoons lemon juice
salt and pepper

1 Scrub the potatoes and place them on a cookie sheet. Prick the potatoes all over with a fork and rub the vegetable oil and salt into their skins.

2 Cook in a preheated oven at 400°F for 1 hour, or until they are soft.

3 Cut the potatoes in half lengthwise and scoop out the flesh, leaving a ¹/2-inch thick shell. Put the shells, skin side uppermost, in the oven for 10 minutes until crisp.

4 Mix the ingredients for the bean sprout salad in a bowl, tossing in the soy sauce, honey, and garlic to coat.

5 Mix the ingredients for the bean filling in a separate bowl.

6 Mix the sour cream and chives in another bowl.

7 Serve the potato skins hot, with the two salad fillings, garnished with snipped chives, together with the sour cream and chive sauce.

Tomato, Olive, & Mozzarella Bruschetta

*These simple toasts are filled with color and flavor. They are great
as a speedy starter or delicious as an appetizer with a good red wine.*

Serves 4

INGREDIENTS

4 muffins
4 garlic cloves, crushed
2 tablespoons butter
1 tablespoon chopped basil
4 large, ripe tomatoes
1 tablespoon tomato paste

8 pitted black olives, halved
1³/4 oz mozzarella
  cheese, sliced
salt and pepper
fresh basil leaves, to garnish

DRESSING:
1 tablespoon olive oil
2 teaspoons lemon juice
1 teaspoon clear honey

1 Cut the muffins in half to give eight thick pieces. Toast the muffin halves under a preheated broiler for 2–3 minutes, until golden.

2 Mix the garlic, butter, and basil together and spread onto each muffin half.

3 Cut a cross shape at the base of each tomato. Plunge the tomatoes in a bowl of boiling water—this will make the skin easier to peel. After a few minutes,

pick each tomato up with a fork and peel away the skin. Chop the tomato flesh and mix with the tomato paste and olives. Divide the mixture between the muffins.

4 Mix the dressing ingredients and drizzle over each muffin. Arrange the mozzarella cheese on top and season to taste with salt and pepper.

5 Return the muffins to the broiler for 1–2 minutes, until the cheese melts.

6 Garnish with fresh basil leaves and serve at once.

VARIATION

Use balsamic vinegar instead of the lemon juice for an authentic Mediterranean flavor.

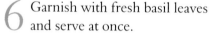

Lentil Pâté

*Red lentils are used in this spicy recipe for speed, as they do not require presoaking.
If you have other lentils, soak, and precook them and use instead of the red lentils.*

Serves 4

INGREDIENTS

1 tablespoon vegetable oil, plus extra
   for greasing
1 onion, chopped
2 garlic cloves, crushed
1 teaspoon garam masala

$^1/_2$ teaspoon ground coriander
$1^1/_4$ cups vegetable stock
$^3/_4$ cup red lentils
1 small egg
2 tablespoons milk

2 tablespoons mango chutney
2 tablespoons chopped parsley, plus
   extra to garnish
salad greens and warm toast,
   to serve

1 Heat the oil in a large saucepan and sauté the onion and garlic for 2–3 minutes, stirring. Add the spices and cook for a further 30 seconds.

2 Stir in the stock and lentils and bring the mixture to a boil. Reduce the heat and simmer for 20 minutes, until the lentils are cooked and softened. Remove the pan from the heat and drain off any excess moisture.

3 Put the mixture in a food processor and add the egg, milk, mango chutney, and 2 tablespoons parsley. Process until completely smooth.

4 Grease and line the base of a 1-pound loaf pan and spoon the mixture into it, leveling and smoothing the surface. Cover and cook in a preheated oven at 400°F for 40–45 minutes, or until the pâté is firm to the touch.

5 Allow the pâté to cool in the pan for about 20 minutes, then transfer to the refrigerator to cool completely.

6 Turn out the pâté onto a serving plate, slice, and garnish with chopped parsley. Serve with salad greens and toast.

VARIATION

Use other spices, such as chili powder or Chinese five-spice powder, to flavor the pâté and add tomato relish or chili relish instead of the mango chutney, if desired.

Roasted Vegetables on Muffins

Roasted vegetables are delicious and attractive. Served on warm muffins with a herb sauce, they are unbeatable.

Serves 4

INGREDIENTS

1 red onion, cut into eight pieces
1 eggplant, halved
　and sliced
1 yellow bell pepper, sliced
1 zucchini, sliced
4 tablespoons olive oil
1 tablespoon garlic vinegar
2 tablespoons vermouth

2 garlic cloves, crushed
1 tablespoon chopped thyme
2 teaspoons light brown sugar
4 muffins, halved
salt and pepper

SAUCE:
2 tablespoons butter
1 tablespoon flour
$2/3$ cup milk
$1/3$ cup vegetable stock
$3/4$ cup grated vegetarian
　Cheddar cheese
1 teaspoon whole-grain mustard
3 tablespoons chopped mixed herbs

1 Arrange the vegetables in a shallow ovenproof dish. Mix together the oil, vinegar, vermouth, garlic, thyme, and sugar and pour over the vegetables, tossing well to coat. Marinate for 1 hour.

2 Transfer the vegetables to a cookie sheet. Cook in a preheated oven at 400°F for 20–25 minutes, or until the vegetables have softened.

3 Meanwhile, make the sauce. Melt the butter in a small pan and add the flour. Cook for 1 minute and remove from the heat. Stir in the milk and stock and return the pan to the heat. Bring to a boil, stirring, until thickened. Stir in the cheese, mustard, and mixed herbs and season well.

4 Preheat the broiler. Cut the muffins in half and broil for 2–3 minutes, until golden brown,

then remove, and arrange on a warm serving plate.

5 Spoon the roasted vegetables onto the muffins and pour the sauce over the top. Serve at once.

Hummus & Garlic Toasts

Hummus is a real favorite spread on these garlic toasts for a delicious starter or as part of a light lunch.

Serves 4

INGREDIENTS

HUMMUS:
14 oz can garbanzo beans
juice of 1 large lemon
6 tablespoons sesame seed paste
2 tablespoons olive oil
2 garlic cloves, crushed

salt and pepper
chopped fresh cilantro and black
olives, to garnish

TOASTS:
1 Italian loaf, sliced
2 garlic cloves, crushed
1 tablespoon chopped fresh cilantro
4 tablespoons olive oil

1 To make the hummus, drain the garbanzo beans, reserving a little of the liquid from the can. Put the garbanzo beans and reserved liquid in a food processor and process, gradually adding the lemon juice. Process well after each addition until the mixture is smooth.

2 Stir in the sesame seed paste and all but 1 teaspoon of the olive oil. Add the garlic, season to taste with salt and pepper and process again until smooth.

3 Spoon the hummus into a serving dish. Drizzle the remaining olive oil over the top and garnish with chopped cilantro and olives. Chill in the refrigerator while you are preparing the toasts.

4 Lay the slices of Italian bread on a broiler rack in a single layer.

5 Mix the garlic, cilantro, and olive oil together and drizzle the mixture over the bread slices. Cook under a preheated broiler for

2–3 minutes, until golden brown, turning once. Serve at once with the hummus.

COOK'S TIP

Make the hummus 1 day in advance, and chill, covered, in the refrigerator until required. Garnish and serve.

Mixed Bean Pâté

This is a really quick starter to prepare if canned beans are used.
Choose a wide variety of beans for color and flavor or use a can of mixed beans.

Serves 4

INGREDIENTS

14 oz can mixed beans,
  drained
2 tablespoons olive oil
juice of 1 lemon
2 garlic cloves, crushed

1 tablespoon chopped fresh cilantro
2 scallions, chopped
salt and pepper

shredded scallions,
  to garnish

1 Rinse the beans thoroughly under cold running water and drain well.

2 Transfer the beans to a food processor or blender and process until smooth. Alternatively, place the beans in a bowl and mash with a fork or potato masher.

3 Add the olive oil, lemon juice, crushed garlic, chopped cilantro, and scallions and process or mix thoroughly until fairly smooth. Season with salt and pepper to taste.

4 Transfer the pâté to a serving bowl and chill for at least 30 minutes. Garnish with shredded scallions and serve at once.

COOK'S TIP

Use canned beans which have no salt or sugar added and always rinse thoroughly before use.

COOK'S TIP

Serve the pâté with warm pita bread or toast.

Vegetable Fritters with Sweet & Sour Sauce

These mixed vegetable fritters are coated in a light batter and deep-fried until golden for a deliciously crisp coating. They are ideal with the sweet and sour dipping sauce.

Serves 4

INGREDIENTS

$^3/_4$ cup whole-wheat flour
pinch of salt
pinch of cayenne pepper
4 teaspoons olive oil
$^3/_4$ cup cold water
$3^1/_2$ oz broccoli florets
$3^1/_2$ oz cauliflower florets
$1^3/_4$ oz snow peas
1 large carrot, cut into thin sticks

1 red bell pepper, sliced
2 egg whites, beaten
oil, for deep-frying

SAUCE:
$^2/_3$ cup pineapple juice
$^2/_3$ cup vegetable stock
2 tablespoons wine vinegar
2 tablespoons light brown sugar
2 teaspoons cornstarch
2 scallions, chopped

1 Sift the flour and salt into a mixing bowl and add the cayenne pepper. Make a well in the center and gradually beat in the oil and cold water to make a smooth batter.

2 Cook the vegetables in boiling water for 5 minutes and drain well.

3 Whisk the egg whites until they form soft peaks and fold them into the batter.

4 Dip the vegetables into the batter, turning to coat well. Drain off any excess batter. Heat the oil for deep-frying in a deep fat fryer to 350°F or until a cube of bread browns in

30 seconds. Fry the vegetables for 1–2 minutes, in batches, until golden. Remove from the oil with a slotted spoon and drain thoroughly on paper towels.

5 Place all the sauce ingredients in a pan and bring to a boil, stirring, until thickened and clear. Serve with the fritters.

Mixed Bhajis

These small bhajis are served in Indian restaurants as accompaniments to a main meal, but they are delicious as a starter with a small salad and yogurt sauce.

Serves 4

INGREDIENTS

BHAJIS:
1¼ cups besan flour*
1 teaspoon baking soda
2 teaspoons ground coriander
1 teaspoon garam masala
1½ teaspoons turmeric
1½ teaspoons chili powder

2 tablespoons chopped cilantro
1 small onion, halved and sliced
1 small leek, sliced
3½ oz cooked cauliflower
9-12 tablespoons cold water
salt and pepper
vegetable oil, for deep-frying

SAUCE:
⅔ cup unsweetened yogurt
2 tablespoons chopped mint
½ teaspoon turmeric
1 garlic clove, crushed
fresh mint sprigs, to garnish

1 Sift the flour, baking soda, and salt to taste into a large mixing bowl and add the spices and chopped fresh cilantro. Mix well until the ingredients are thoroughly combined.

2 Divide the mixture into 3 separate bowls. Stir the onion into one bowl, the leek into another, and the cauliflower into the third. Add 3–4 tablespoons of water to each bowl and mix each to form a smooth paste.

3 Heat the oil for deep-frying in a deep fat fryer to 350°F or until a cube of bread browns in 30 seconds. Using 2 dessert spoons, form the mixture into rounds and cook each in the oil for 3–4 minutes, until browned. Remove with a slotted spoon and drain on absorbent paper towels. Keep the bhajis warm in the oven while cooking the remainder.

4 Mix all of the sauce ingredients together and pour into a serving bowl. Garnish with mint sprigs and serve with the warm bhajis.

VARIATION

*Use cooked broccoli instead of the cauliflower or cooked spinach instead of the leek. *Besan is a chickpea flour available in specialty health food and Middle Eastern markets.*

Mushroom & Garlic Soufflés

These individual soufflés are very impressive starters, but must be cooked just before serving to prevent them from sinking.

Serves 4

INGREDIENTS

4 tablespoons butter
1 cup chopped flat mushrooms
2 teaspoons lime juice
2 garlic cloves, crushed

2 tablespoons chopped marjoram
3 tablespoons all-purpose flour
1 cup milk

salt and pepper
2 eggs, separated

1 Lightly grease the inside of four ⅔-cup individual soufflé dishes with a little butter.

2 Melt 2 tablespoons of the butter in a skillet. Add the mushrooms, lime juice, and garlic and sauté for 2–3 minutes. Remove the mushroom mixture from the skillet with a slotted spoon and transfer to a mixing bowl. Stir in the marjoram.

3 Melt the remaining butter in a pan. Add the flour and cook for 1 minute, then remove from the heat. Stir in the milk and return to the heat. Bring to a boil, stirring until thickened.

4 Add the sauce to the mushroom mixture, mixing well, and beat in the egg yolks.

5 Whisk the egg whites until they form peaks and gently fold into the mushroom mixture until fully incorporated.

6 Divide the mixture among the prepared soufflé dishes. Place the dishes on a cookie sheet and cook in a preheated oven at 400°F for 8–10 minutes, or until the soufflés have risen and are cooked through and golden brown on top. Serve at once.

COOK'S TIP

Insert a toothpick into the center of the soufflés to test if they are cooked through—it should come out clean. If not, cook for a few minutes longer, but do not overcook, otherwise they will become rubbery.

Carrot, Fennel, & Potato Medley

This is a colorful dish of shredded vegetables in a fresh garlic and honey dressing.
It is delicious served with crusty bread to mop up the dressing.

Serves 4

INGREDIENTS

2 tablespoons olive oil
1 potato, cut into thin strips
1 fennel bulb, cut into thin strips
2 carrots, grated
1 red onion, cut into thin strips
chopped chives and fennel fronds,
   to garnish

DRESSING:
3 tablespoons olive oil
1 tablespoon garlic wine vinegar
1 garlic clove, crushed
1 teaspoon Dijon mustard
2 teaspoons clear honey
salt and pepper

1 Heat the olive oil in a skillet, add the potato and fennel slices, and cook for 2–3 minutes, until beginning to brown. Remove the vegetables from the skillet with a slotted spoon and drain on paper towels.

2 Arrange the carrot, red onion, potato, and fennel in separate piles on a serving platter.

3 Mix the dressing ingredients together and pour over the vegetables. Toss well and sprinkle with chopped chives and fennel fronds. Serve immediately or leave in the refrigerator until required.

VARIATION

Use mixed, broiled bell peppers or shredded leeks in this dish for variety, or add bean sprouts and a segmented orange, if desired.

COOK'S TIP

Fennel is an aromatic plant that has a delicate, aniseed flavor. It can be eaten raw in salads, or boiled, braised, sautéed, or broiled. For this salad, if fennel is unavailable, substitute 12 ounces sliced leeks.

Onions à la Grecque

This is a well-known method of cooking vegetables and is perfect with shallots or onions, served with a crisp salad.

Serves 4

INGREDIENTS

1 pound shallots
3 tablespoons olive oil
3 tablespoons clear honey
2 tablespoons garlic wine vinegar
3 tablespoons dry white wine
1 tablespoon tomato paste

2 celery stalks, sliced
2 tomatoes, seeded and chopped
salt and pepper
chopped celery leaves, to garnish

1 Peel the shallots. Heat the oil in a large saucepan, add the shallots, and cook, stirring, for 3–5 minutes, or until they begin to brown.

2 Add the honey and cook for a further 30 seconds over a high heat, then add the garlic wine vinegar and dry white wine, stirring well.

3 Stir in the tomato paste, celery, and tomatoes and bring the mixture to a boil. Cook over a high heat for 5–6 minutes. Season to taste and set aside to cool slightly.

4 Garnish with chopped celery leaves and serve warm or cold from the refrigerator.

COOK'S TIP

This dish, served warm, would also make an ideal accompaniment to Garbanzo Bean Roast (page 114).

VARIATION

Use button mushrooms instead of the shallots and fennel instead of the celery for another great starter.

Eggplant Timbale

This is a great way to serve pasta as a starter, wrapped in an eggplant mold. It looks really impressive, yet it is so easy to make.

Serves 4

INGREDIENTS

1 large eggplant
1/2 cup macaroni
1 tablespoon vegetable oil
1 onion, chopped
2 garlic cloves, crushed
2 tablespoons drained
    canned corn
2 tablespoons frozen peas, thawed

3 1/2 ounces spinach
1/4 cup grated vegetarian
    Cheddar cheese
1 egg, beaten
3 cups canned, chopped tomatoes
1 tablespoon chopped basil
salt and pepper

SAUCE:
4 tablespoons olive oil
2 tablespoons white wine vinegar
2 garlic cloves, crushed
3 tablespoons chopped basil
1 tablespoon superfine sugar

1 Cut the eggplant lengthwise into thin strips, using a swivel vegetable peeler. Place them in a bowl of salted boiling water and let stand for about 3–4 minutes. Drain well.

2 Lightly grease the base and sides of four 2/3-cup individual ramekin dishes and use the eggplant slices to line the dishes, leaving about 1 inch of eggplant overlapping.

3 Cook the pasta in a pan of boiling water for 8–10 minutes until "al dente." Drain. Heat the oil in a pan and sauté the onion and garlic for 2–3 minutes. Stir in the corn and peas and remove from the heat.

4 Blanch the spinach, drain well, chop, and reserve. Add the pasta to the onion mixture with the cheese, egg, tomatoes, and basil. Season and mix. Half fill

each ramekin with some of the pasta. Spoon the spinach on top, and then the remaining pasta mixture. Fold the eggplant over the pasta filling to cover. Put the ramekins in a roasting pan half-filled with boiling water, cover, and cook in a preheated oven at 350°F for 20–25 minutes, or until set. Meanwhile, heat the sauce ingredients in a pan. Turn out the ramekins and serve at once with the sauce.

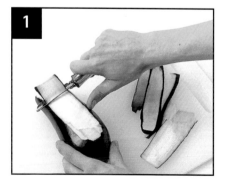

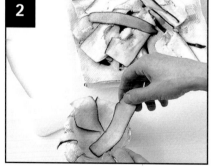

Snacks & Light Meals

The ability to rustle up a simple snack or a quickly prepared light meal can be very important in our busy lives. Sometimes we may not feel like eating a full-scale meal but nonetheless want something appetizing and satisfying. Or if lunch or dinner is going to be served very late, then we may want something to tide us over. Whether it is for a sustaining snack to break the day, hearty appetizers to serve with predinner drinks, or a first course for an informal lunch or supper party, you'll find a mouth-watering collection of recipes in this chapter. They cater to all tastes and times of day, and many can be prepared ahead of time and will not detain you in the kitchen for too long.

There are many easy-to-prepare dishes in this chapter, which will satisfy your hunger as well as your taste-buds, with hardly a sandwich in sight! You will easily find something to sustain you that is lighter than the main dish meals in the following chapter, but may also be served with an accompaniment or crisp salad, a selection of which you will find later in the book.

Garlic Mushrooms on Toast

This is so simple to prepare and looks great if you use a variety of mushrooms for shape and texture. Cooked in garlic butter, they are simply irresistible.

Serves 4

INGREDIENTS

6 tablespoons vegetarian margarine

2 garlic cloves, crushed

4 cups sliced mixed mushrooms, such as open-cap, button, oyster, and shiitake

8 slices French bread

1 tablespoon chopped parsley

salt and pepper

1 Melt the margarine in a skillet over medium heat. Add the crushed garlic and cook for 30 seconds, stirring.

2 Add the mushrooms and cook for 5 minutes, turning occasionally.

3 Toast the slices of French bread under a preheated broiler for about 2–3 minutes, turning once.

4 Transfer the toasts to a serving plate.

5 Toss the parsley into the mushrooms, mixing well, and season well with salt and pepper to taste.

6 Spoon the mushroom mixture over the bread and serve at once.

COOK'S TIP

Add seasonings, such as curry powder or chili powder, to the mushrooms for extra flavor, if desired.

COOK'S TIP

Store mushrooms for 24–36 hours in the refrigerator, in paper bags, as they sweat in plastic. Exotic mushrooms should be washed, but other varieties can simply be wiped with paper towels.

Potato, Bell Pepper, & Mushroom Hash

This is a quick one-pan dish that is ideal for a quick snack. Packed with color and flavor, it is very versatile and you can add any other vegetable you have at hand.

Serves 4

INGREDIENTS

1½ pounds potatoes, cubed
1 tablespoon olive oil
2 garlic cloves, crushed
1 green bell pepper, cubed
1 yellow bell pepper, cubed

3 tomatoes, diced
1 cup halved button mushrooms
1 tablespoon vegetarian
  Worcestershire sauce
2 tablespoons chopped basil

salt and pepper
fresh basil sprigs, to garnish
warm, crusty bread, to serve

1 Cook the potatoes in a saucepan of boiling, salted water for 7–8 minutes. Drain well and reserve.

2 Heat the olive oil in a large, heavy-based skillet and cook the potatoes for 8–10 minutes, stirring constantly, until they are golden brown.

3 Add the garlic and bell peppers and cook for 2–3 minutes.

4 Stir in the tomatoes and mushrooms and cook, stirring, for 5–6 minutes.

5 Stir in the vegetarian Worcestershire sauce and basil and season well. Garnish and serve with crusty bread.

VARIATION

This dish can also be eaten cold as a salad.

COOK'S TIP

Most brands of Worcestershire sauce contain anchovies, so make sure you choose a vegetarian variety.

Vegetable Samosas

*These Indian snacks are perfect for a quick or light meal,
served with a salad. They can be made in advance and frozen for ease.*

Makes 12

INGREDIENTS

FILLING:
2 tablespoons vegetable oil
1 onion, chopped
$^1/_2$ teaspoon ground coriander
$^1/_2$ teaspoon ground cumin
pinch of turmeric

$^1/_2$ teaspoon ground ginger
$^1/_2$ teaspoon garam masala
1 garlic clove, crushed
$1^1/_2$ cups diced potatoes
1 cup frozen peas, thawed
2 cups chopped spinach

PASTRY:
12 sheets filo pastry
oil, for deep-frying

1 To make the filling, heat the oil in a skillet and sauté the onion for 1–2 minutes, stirring constantly, until softened. Stir in all of the spices and garlic and cook for 1 minute.

2 Add the potatoes and cook over gentle heat for 5 minutes, stirring, until they begin to soften.

3 Stir in the peas and spinach and cook for a further 3–4 minutes.

4 Lay the filo pastry sheets out on a clean counter and fold each sheet in half lengthwise.

5 Place 2 tablespoons of the vegetable filling at one end of each folded pastry sheet. Fold over one corner to make a triangle. Continue folding the pastry in this way to make a triangular packet and then seal the edges by brushing with a little water.

6 Repeat with the remaining pastry and filling.

7 Heat the oil for deep-frying to 350°F or until a cube of bread browns in 30 seconds. Fry the samosas, in batches, for 1–2 minutes, until golden. Drain on absorbent paper towels and keep warm while cooking the remainder. Serve at once.

COOK'S TIP

*Serve with a yogurt sauce
(see page 44) and a salad.*

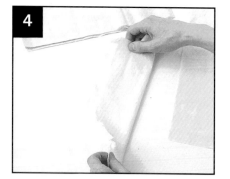

Scrambled Bean Curd on Toasted Rolls

This is a delicious dish that would also serve as a light lunch or supper.

Serves 4

INGREDIENTS

6 tablespoons vegetarian margarine
1 pound marinated,
  firm bean curd
1 red onion, chopped

1 red bell pepper, chopped
4 rolls
2 tablespoons chopped mixed herbs
salt and pepper

fresh herbs, to garnish

1 Melt the margarine in a heavy-based skillet over medium heat and crumble the bean curd into the pan.

2 Add the onion and bell pepper and cook for 3–4 minutes, stirring occasionally.

3 Meanwhile, slice the rolls in half and toast under a preheated broiler for about 2–3 minutes, turning once. Remove the toasts and transfer to a serving plate.

4 Add the herbs to the bean curd mixture, combine, and season to taste.

5 Spoon the bean curd mixture onto the toast and garnish with fresh herbs. Serve at once.

COOK'S TIP

Marinated bean curd adds extra flavor to this dish. Smoked bean curd could be used in its place.

COOK'S TIP

Rub the cut surface of a garlic clove over the toasted rolls for extra flavor.

Mixed Bean Pan-Fry

Fresh green beans have a wonderful flavor that is hard to beat.
If you cannot find fresh beans, use thawed, frozen beans instead.

Serves 4

INGREDIENTS

4 cups mixed fresh beans, such as
  green and fava beans
2 tablespoons vegetable oil
2 garlic cloves, crushed
1 red onion, halved
  and sliced

8 ounces firm marinated
  bean curd, diced
1 tablespoon lemon juice
$1/2$ teaspoon turmeric
1 teaspoon pumpkin pie spice

$2/3$ cup vegetable stock
2 teaspoons sesame seeds

1 Trim and chop the green beans and set aside until they are required.

2 Heat the oil in a skillet over medium heat and sauté the garlic and onion for 2 minutes, stirring well.

3 Add the bean curd and cook for 2–3 minutes, until it is just beginning to brown.

4 Add the green beans and fava beans. Stir in the lemon juice, turmeric, pumpkin pie spice, and vegetable stock and bring to a boil.

5 Reduce the heat and simmer for 5–7 minutes, or until the beans are tender. Sprinkle with sesame seeds and serve at once.

VARIATION

Add lime juice instead of lemon, for an alternative citrus flavor.

VARIATION

Use smoked bean curd instead of marinated bean curd for an alternative flavor.

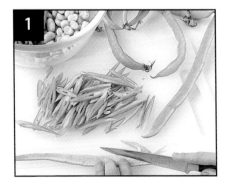

Calzone with Sun-dried Tomatoes & Vegetables

These pizza base parcels are great for making in advance and freezing—they can be thawed when required for a quick snack.

Makes 4

INGREDIENTS

DOUGH:
3 1/2 cups all-purpose flour
2 teaspoons active yeast
1 teaspoon superfine sugar
2/3 cup vegetable stock
2/3 cup sieved tomatoes
beaten egg

FILLING:
1 tablespoon vegetable oil
1 onion, chopped
1 garlic clove, crushed
2 tablespoons chopped sun-dried tomatoes
1 cup chopped spinach
3 tablespoons canned and drained corn

1/4 cup green beans, cut into three pieces
1 tablespoon tomato paste
1 tablespoon chopped oregano
2 ounces mozzarella cheese, sliced
salt and pepper

1 Sift the flour into a bowl. Add the active dry yeast and sugar and then beat in the stock and sieved tomatoes to make a smooth dough.

2 Knead the dough on a lightly floured counter for 10 minutes, then place in a clean, lightly oiled bowl and set aside to rise in a warm place for 1 hour.

3 Heat the oil in a skillet and sauté the onion for about 2–3 minutes. Stir in the garlic, tomatoes, spinach, corn, and beans and cook for 3–4 minutes. Add the tomato paste and oregano and season well.

4 Divide the risen dough into 4 equal portions and roll each onto a floured surface to form a

7-inch round. Spoon a quarter of the filling onto one half of each round and top with cheese. Fold the dough over to encase the filling, sealing the edge with a fork. Glaze with beaten egg. Put the calzone on a lightly greased cookie sheet and cook in a preheated oven at 425°F for 25–30 minutes, until risen and golden. Transfer to warm plates and serve.

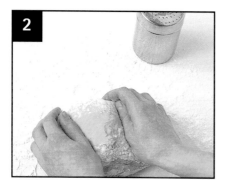

Vegetable Enchiladas

This Mexican dish uses prepared tortillas, which are readily available in supermarkets.
They are filled with a spicy vegetable mixture and topped with a hot tomato sauce.

Serves 4

INGREDIENTS

4 flour tortillas
$3/4$ cup grated vegetarian
   Cheddar cheese

FILLING:
$2^3/4$ ounces spinach
2 tablespoons olive oil
8 baby corn cobs, sliced
1 tablespoon frozen peas, thawed

1 red bell pepper, diced
1 carrot, diced
1 leek, sliced
2 garlic cloves, crushed
1 red chili, chopped
salt and pepper

SAUCE:
$1^1/4$ cups sieved tomatoes
2 shallots, chopped
1 garlic clove, crushed
$1^1/4$ cups vegetable stock
1 teaspoon superfine sugar
1 teaspoon chili powder

1 To make the filling, blanch the spinach in a pan of boiling water for 2 minutes, drain well, and chop.

2 Heat the oil in a heavy-based skillet and sauté the corn, peas, bell pepper, carrot, leek, garlic, and chili for 3–4 minutes, stirring briskly. Stir in the spinach and season well with salt and pepper to taste.

3 Put all of the sauce ingredients in a saucepan and bring to a boil, stirring. Cook over a high heat for 20 minutes, stirring constantly, until thickened and reduced by a third.

4 Spoon a quarter of the filling along the center of each tortilla. Roll the tortillas around the filling and place in an ovenproof dish, seam side down.

5 Pour the sauce over the tortillas and sprinkle the cheese on top. Cook in a preheated oven at 350°F for 20 minutes, or until the cheese has melted and browned. Serve at once.

Spinach Gnocchi with Tomato & Basil Sauce

These gnocchi or small dumplings are made with potatoes and flavored with spinach and nutmeg, and served in a rich tomato sauce for an ideal light meal.

Serves 4

INGREDIENTS

1 pound baking potatoes
2³/₄ ounces spinach
1 teaspoon water
3 tablespoons butter or
   vegetarian margarine
1 small egg, beaten

³/₄ cup plain all-purpose flour
fresh basil sprigs, to garnish

TOMATO SAUCE:
1 tablespoon olive oil
1 shallot, chopped
1 tablespoon tomato paste

8 ounce can chopped tomatoes
2 tablespoons chopped basil
6 tablespoons red wine
1 teaspoon sugar
salt and pepper

1 Cook the potatoes in their skins in a pan of boiling salted water for 20 minutes. Drain well and press through a strainer into a bowl. Cook the spinach in 1 teaspoon water for 5 minutes, until wilted. Drain and pat dry with paper towels. Chop and stir into the potatoes.

2 Add the butter or margarine, egg, and half of the flour to the potato mixture, mixing well.

Turn out onto a floured counter, gradually kneading in the remaining flour to form a soft dough. With floured hands, roll the dough into thin ropes and cut off ³/₄-inch pieces. Press the center of each dumpling with your finger, drawing it toward you to curl the sides of the gnocchi. Cover and set aside to chill.

3 Heat the oil for the sauce in a pan and sauté the chopped

shallots for 5 minutes. Add the tomato paste, tomatoes, basil, red wine, and sugar and season well. Bring to a boil and then simmer for 20 minutes.

4 Bring a pan of salted water to a boil and cook the gnocchi for 2–3 minutes, or until they rise to the top of the pan. Drain well and transfer to serving dishes. Spoon the tomato sauce over the top. Garnish and serve.

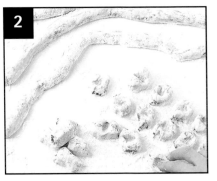

Vegetable Jambalaya

*This dish traditionally contains spicy sausage, but it is equally delicious
filled with vegetables in this spicy vegetarian version.*

Serves 4

INGREDIENTS

$^1/_2$ cup brown rice
2 tablespoons olive oil
2 garlic cloves, crushed
1 red onion, cut into eight wedges
1 eggplant, diced
1 green bell pepper, diced

$^1/_2$ cup baby corn cobs,
  halved lengthwise
$^1/_2$ cup frozen peas
$3^1/_2$ ounces small broccoli florets
$^2/_3$ cup vegetable stock
8 ounce can chopped tomatoes

1 tablespoon tomato paste
1 teaspoon Creole seasoning
$^1/_2$ teaspoon chili flakes
salt and pepper

1 Cook the rice in a saucepan of boiling water for 20 minutes, or until cooked through. Drain and set aside.

2 Heat the oil in a heavy-based skillet. Add the garlic and onion and fry, stirring constantly, for 2–3 minutes.

3 Add the eggplant, bell pepper, corn, peas, and broccoli florets to the skillet and cook, stirring occasionally, for about 2–3 minutes.

4 Stir in the vegetable stock and canned tomatoes, tomato paste, Creole seasoning, and chili flakes.

5 Season to taste and cook over low heat for 15–20 minutes, or until the vegetables are tender.

6 Stir the brown rice into the vegetable mixture and cook, mixing well, for 3–4 minutes, or until hot. Transfer the vegetable jambalaya to warm serving dishes and serve at once.

COOK'S TIP

Use a mixture of rice, such as wild or red rice, for color and texture. Cook the rice in advance for a speedier recipe.

Stuffed Mushrooms

Use large open-cap mushrooms for this recipe
for their flavor and suitability for filling.

Serves 4

INGREDIENTS

8 open-cap mushrooms
1 tablespoon olive oil
1 small leek, chopped
1 celery stalk, chopped
$3^1/_2$ ounces bean
   curd, diced
1 zucchini, chopped

1 carrot, chopped
1 cup whole-wheat bread crumbs
2 tablespoons chopped basil
1 tablespoon tomato paste
2 tablespoons pine nuts

$^3/_4$ cup grated vegetarian
   cheddar cheese
$^2/_3$ cup vegetable stock
salt and pepper
salad greens, to serve

1 Remove the stalks from the mushrooms and chop finely. Reserve the caps.

2 Heat the oil in a heavy-based skillet. Add the chopped mushroom stalks, leek, celery, bean curd, zucchini, and carrot and cook for 3–4 minutes, stirring.

3 Stir in the bread crumbs, basil, tomato paste, and pine nuts. Season with salt and pepper to taste.

4 Spoon the mixture into the mushroom caps and top with the grated cheese.

5 Place the mushrooms in a shallow ovenproof dish and pour the vegetable stock around them.

6 Cook in a preheated oven at 425°F for 20 minutes, or until the mushroom caps and stuffing are cooked through and the cheese has melted. Remove the

mushrooms from the dish and serve at once with salad greens.

COOK'S TIP

Vary the vegetables used
for flavor and color or
according to those you
have available.

Vegetable Crêpes

Crêpes are ideal for filling with your favorite ingredients. In this recipe, they are packed with a spicy vegetable filling which may be made in advance and heated through for serving.

Serves 4

INGREDIENTS

CRÊPES:
3/4 cup all-purpose flour
pinch of salt
1 egg, beaten
1 1/4 cups milk
vegetable oil, for frying

FILLING:
2 tablespoons vegetable oil
1 leek, shredded
1/2 teaspoon chili powder
1/2 teaspoon ground cumin
1 3/4 ounces snow peas
3 1/2 ounces button mushrooms,
1 red bell pepper, sliced
1/4 cup cashew nuts, chopped

SAUCE:
2 tablespoons vegetarian margarine
3 tablespoons all-purpose flour
2/3 cup vegetable stock
2/3 cup milk
1 teaspoon Dijon mustard
3/4 cup grated vegetarian
   cheddar cheese,
2 tablespoons chopped cilantro

1 For the crêpes, sift the flour and salt into a bowl. Beat in the egg and milk to make a batter. For the filling, heat the oil in a skillet and sauté the leek for 2–3 minutes. Add the rest of the ingredients and cook for 5 minutes, stirring. To make the sauce, melt the margarine in a pan and add the flour. Cook for 1 minute and remove from the heat. Stir in the stock and milk and return to the heat. Bring to a boil, stirring until thick. Add the mustard, half the cheese, and the cilantro and cook for 1 minute.

2 Heat 1 tablespoon of oil in a nonstick 6-inch skillet. Pour the oil from the pan and add an eighth of the batter, to cover the base of the skillet. Cook for 2 minutes, turn the crêpe, and cook the other side for 1 minute. Repeat with the remaining batter. Spoon a little of the filling along the center of each crêpe and roll up. Place in a heatproof dish and pour the sauce on top. Top with cheese and heat under a preheated broiler for 3–5 minutes, or until the cheese melts and turns golden. Serve at once.

Vegetable Pasta Nests

*These large pasta nests look impressive when presented filled
with broiled mixed vegetables and taste delicious.*

Serves 4

INGREDIENTS

6 ounces spaghetti
1 eggplant, halved and sliced
1 zucchini, diced
1 red bell pepper, seeded and
    sliced diagonally
6 tablespoons olive oil

2 garlic cloves, crushed
4 tablespoons butter or
    vegetarian margarine, melted
1 tablespoon dry white bread crumbs
salt and pepper
fresh parsley sprigs, to garnish

1 Bring a large saucepan of
water to a boil and cook the
spaghetti until "al dente," or
according to the instructions on
the packet. Drain well and set
aside until required.

2 Place the eggplant, zucchini,
and bell pepper in a single
layer on a cookie sheet.

3 Mix the oil and garlic
together and pour the
mixture over the vegetables,
tossing to coat.

4 Cook under a preheated
broiler for about 10 minutes,
turning frequently, until tender
and lightly charred. Set aside and
keep warm.

5 Divide the spaghetti among
4 lightly greased muffin pans.
Using a fork, curl the spaghetti to
form nests.

6 Brush the pasta nests with
melted butter or margarine
and sprinkle with the bread
crumbs. Bake in a preheated oven,

at 400°F for 15 minutes, or until
lightly golden. Remove the pasta
nests from the pans and transfer to
serving plates. Divide the broiled
vegetables among the pasta nests,
season, and garnish.

COOK'S TIP

*"Al dente" means to the bite and
describes cooked pasta that is not too
soft, but still has a bite to it.*

Vegetable Burgers & Fries

These spicy vegetable burgers are delicious, especially when served with the light oven fries. Serve them in a warm hamburger bun with radicchio leaves and red onion relish.

Serves 4

INGREDIENTS

VEGETABLE BURGERS:
3$^1/_2$ ounces spinach
1 tablespoon olive oil
1 leek, chopped
2 garlic cloves, crushed
1$^1/_2$ cups chopped mushrooms
10$^1/_2$ ounces firm bean
  curd, chopped

1 teaspoon chili powder
1 teaspoon curry powder
1 tablespoon chopped cilantro
1$^1/_2$ cups fresh whole-wheat
  bread crumbs
1 tablespoon olive oil

FRIES:
2 large potatoes
2 tablespoons all-purpose flour
1 teaspoon chili powder
2 tablespoons olive oil
hamburger bun and salad, to serve

1 To make the burgers, cook the spinach in a little water for 2 minutes. Drain thoroughly and pat dry with paper towels.

2 Heat the oil in a skillet and sauté the leek and garlic for 2–3 minutes. Add the remaining ingredients, except for the bread crumbs, and cook for about 5–7 minutes, until the vegetables have softened. Toss in the spinach and cook for 1 minute.

3 Transfer the mixture to a food processor and process for 30 seconds, until almost smooth. Stir in the bread crumbs, mixing well, and set aside until cool enough to handle. Using floured hands, form the mixture into four equal-size burgers. Chill in the refrigerator for 30 minutes.

4 To make the fries, cut the potatoes into thin wedges and cook in a pan of boiling water for

10 minutes. Drain thoroughly and toss in the flour and chili powder. Spread out the fries on a cookie sheet and sprinkle with the oil. Cook in a preheated oven at 400°F for 30 minutes, or until cooked through and golden brown.

5 Meanwhile, heat the olive oil in a skillet and cook the burgers over medium heat for 8–10 minutes, turning once. Serve in a hamburger bun with a salad.

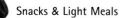
Vegetable Dim Sum

Dim sum are small Chinese packets, usually served as part of a large mixed meal.
They may be filled with any variety of fillings, steamed or fried, and served with a dipping sauce.

Serves 4

INGREDIENTS

2 scallions, chopped
1 ounce green beans, chopped
$1/2$ small carrot, finely chopped
1 red chili, chopped
$1/3$ cup bean sprouts,
   chopped

$1/3$ cup chopped button mushrooms
$1/4$ cup unsalted cashew
   nuts, chopped
1 small egg, beaten
2 tablespoons cornstarch
1 teaspoon light soy sauce

1 teaspoon hoisin sauce
1 teaspoon sesame oil
32 wonton wrappers
oil, for deep-frying
1 tablespoon sesame seeds

1 Mix all of the vegetables together in a bowl.

2 Add the nuts, egg, cornstarch, soy sauce, hoisin sauce, and sesame oil to the bowl, stirring to mix well.

3 Spread out the wonton wrappers on a chopping board and spoon small quantities of the mixture into the center of each. Gather the wrappers around the filling at the top, to make little parcels, leaving the top open.

4 Heat the oil for deep-frying in a preheated wok to 350°F or until a cube of bread browns in 30 seconds.

5 Fry the wontons, in batches, for 1–2 minutes, or until golden brown. Drain on absorbent paper towels and keep warm while frying the remaining wontons.

6 Sprinkle the sesame seeds over the wontons. Serve the vegetable dim sum with a soy or plum dipping sauce.

COOK'S TIP

If desired, arrange the wontons on a heatproof plate and then steam in a steamer for 5-7 minutes for a healthier cooking method.

Cheese & Garlic Mushroom Pizzas

This pizza dough is flavored with garlic and herbs and topped with mixed mushrooms and melting cheese for a really delicious pizza.

Serves 4

INGREDIENTS

DOUGH:
$3^1/2$ cups all-purpose flour
2 teaspoons active dry yeast
2 garlic cloves, crushed
2 tablespoons chopped thyme
2 tablespoons olive oil
$1^1/4$ cups tepid water

TOPPING:
2 tablespoons butter or
  vegetarian margarine
5 cups sliced mixed mushrooms
2 garlic cloves, crushed
2 tablespoons chopped parsley
2 tablespoons tomato paste

6 tablespoons sieved tomatoes
$3/4$ cup grated mozzarella cheese
salt and pepper
chopped parsley, to garnish

1 Put the flour, yeast, garlic, and thyme in a bowl. Make a well in the center and gradually stir in the oil and water. Bring together to form a soft dough.

2 Turn the dough onto a floured counter and knead for 5 minutes, or until smooth. Roll into a 14-inch round and place on a greased cookie sheet. Set aside in a warm place for 20 minutes, or until the dough puffs up.

3 Meanwhile, make the topping. Melt the margarine or butter in a heavy-based skillet and sauté the mushrooms, garlic, and parsley over medium heat for 5 minutes, stirring occasionally.

4 Mix the tomato paste and sieved tomatoes and spoon onto the pizza base, leaving a $1/2$-inch edge of dough. Spoon the mushroom mixture on top. Season well with salt and pepper and sprinkle the cheese on top. Cook the pizza in a preheated oven at 375°F for 20–25 minutes, or until the base is crisp and the cheese has melted. Garnish with chopped parsley and serve.

COOK'S TIP

If desired, spread the base with a prepared cheese sauce before adding the mushrooms.

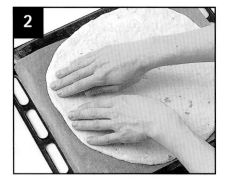

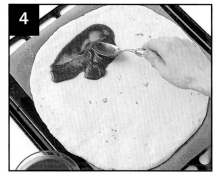

Watercress & Cheese Tartlets

These individual tartlets are great for lunchtime or for picnic food. Watercress is a good source of folic acid, which is important in early pregnancy.

Makes 4

INGREDIENTS

³/₄ cup all-purpose flour
pinch of salt
¹/₂ cup butter or
   vegetarian margarine
2–3 tablespoons cold water
2 bunches watercress

2 garlic cloves, crushed
1 shallot, chopped
1¹/₂ cups grated vegetarian
   cheddar cheese,

4 tablespoons plain yogurt
¹/₂ teaspoons paprika

1 Sift the flour into a mixing bowl and add the salt. Rub ¹/₃ cup of the butter or margarine into the flour until the mixture resembles bread crumbs.

2 Stir in the cold water to make a firm dough.

3 Knead the dough lightly, then roll out on a lightly floured counter and use to line four 4-inch tartlet pans. Prick the bases with a fork and set aside in the refrigerator to chill.

4 Heat the remaining butter or margarine in a skillet. Discard the stems from the watercress and add the leaves to the skillet, together with the garlic and shallot, cooking for 1–2 minutes, until the watercress is wilted.

5 Remove the skillet from the heat and stir in the cheese, yogurt, and paprika.

6 Spoon the mixture into the pastry cases and cook in a preheated oven at 350°F for

20 minutes or until the filling is firm. Turn out the tartlets and serve hot or cold.

VARIATION

Use spinach instead of the watercress, making sure it is well drained before mixing with the remaining filling ingredients.

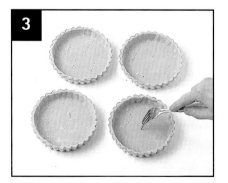

Vegetable-Filled Ravioli

*These small packets are very easy to make and have the advantage of being filled with
your favorite mixture of succulent mushrooms. Serve with freshly grated cheese sprinkled on top.*

Serves 4

INGREDIENTS

FILLING:
3 tablespoons butter or
   vegetarian margarine
2 garlic cloves, crushed
1 small leek, chopped
2 celery stalks, chopped

2¹/₃ cups chopped open-
   cap mushrooms
1 egg, beaten
2 tablespoons grated vegetarian
   Parmesan cheese
salt and pepper

RAVIOLI:
4 sheets filo pastry
3 tablespoons vegetarian margarine
oil, for deep-frying

1 To make the filling, melt the butter or margarine in a heavy-based skillet and sauté the garlic and leek for 2–3 minutes, until softened.

2 Add the celery and mushrooms and cook for a further 4–5 minutes, until all the vegetables are tender.

3 Turn off the heat and stir in the egg and grated Parmesan cheese. Season with salt and pepper to taste.

4 Lay the pastry sheets on a chopping board and cut each into nine squares.

5 Spoon a little of the filling into the center of half the squares and brush the edges of the pastry with butter or margarine. Lay another square on top and seal the edges to make a packet.

6 Heat the oil for deep-frying to 350°F or until a cube of bread browns in 30 seconds. Fry the ravioli, in batches, for about

2–3 minutes, or until golden brown. Remove from the oil with a slotted spoon and pat dry on absorbent paper towels. Transfer to a warm serving plate and serve.

COOK'S TIP

Parmesan cheese is generally non-vegetarian. However, there is an Italian Parmesan called Grano Padano, which is usually vegetarian. Alternatively you could use Pecorino.

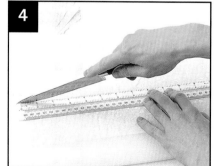

Bulgur-Filled Eggplants

In this recipe, eggplants are filled with a spicy bulgur wheat and vegetable stuffing for a delicious light meal.

Serves 4

INGREDIENTS

4 medium eggplants
salt
$^3/_4$ cup bulgur wheat
$1^1/_4$ cups boiling water
3 tablespoons olive oil
2 garlic cloves, crushed
2 tablespoons pine nuts

$^1/_2$ teaspoons turmeric
1 teaspoon chili powder
2 celery stalks, chopped
4 scallions, chopped
1 carrot, grated

$^3/_4$ cup chopped button mushrooms
2 tablespoons raisins
2 tablespoons chopped fresh cilantro
salad greens, to serve

1 Cut the eggplants in half lengthwise and scoop out the flesh with a teaspoon without piercing the shells. Chop the flesh and set aside. Rub the insides of the eggplants with a little salt and set aside, upside down, for about 20 minutes.

2 Meanwhile, put the bulgur wheat in a mixing bowl and pour the boiling water over the top. Let stand for 20 minutes, or until the water has been absorbed.

3 Heat the oil in a skillet. Add the garlic, pine nuts, turmeric, chili powder, celery, scallions, carrot, mushrooms, and raisins and cook for 2–3 minutes.

4 Stir in the reserved eggplant flesh and cook for a further 2–3 minutes. Add the cilantro, mixing well.

5 Remove the skillet from the heat and stir in the bulgur wheat. Rinse the eggplant shells under cold water and pat dry with paper towels.

6 Spoon the bulgur filling into the eggplants and place in a roasting pan. Pour in a little boiling water and cook in a preheated oven at 350°F for 15–20 minutes.

7 Serve hot with salad greens.

Lentil Croquettes

These croquettes are ideal served with a crisp salad and a sesame seed paste dip.

Serves 4

INGREDIENTS

1¼ cups split red lentils
1 green bell pepper, finely chopped
1 red onion, finely chopped
2 garlic cloves, crushed
1 teaspoon garam masala
½ teaspoon chili powder

1 teaspoon ground cumin
2 teaspoons lemon juice
2 tablespoons chopped
  unsalted peanuts
2½ cups water
1 egg, beaten

3 tablespoons all-purpose flour
1 teaspoon turmeric
1 teaspoon chili powder
4 tablespoons vegetable oil
salt and pepper
salad greens and fresh herbs, to serve

1 Put the lentils in a large saucepan with the bell pepper, onion, garlic, garam masala, chili powder, ground cumin, lemon juice, and peanuts.

2 Add the water and bring to a boil. Reduce the heat and simmer for 30 minutes, or until the liquid has been absorbed, stirring occasionally.

3 Remove the mixture from the heat and let cool slightly. Beat in the egg and season with salt and pepper to taste. Set aside to cool completely.

4 With floured hands, form the mixture into eight oval shapes.

5 Mix the flour, turmeric, and chili powder together on a small plate. Roll the croquettes in the spiced flour mixture to coat.

6 Heat the oil in a large skillet and cook the croquettes, in batches, for 10 minutes, turning once, until they are cooked through and crisp on both sides. Serve the croquettes with salad greens and fresh herbs.

COOK'S TIP

Other lentils could be used, but they will require soaking and precooking before use. Red lentils are used for speed and convenience.

Refried Beans with Tortillas

Refried beans are a classic Mexican dish and are usually served as an accompaniment. They are, however, delicious when served with warm tortillas and a quick onion relish.

Serves 4

INGREDIENTS

BEANS:
2 tablespoons olive oil
1 onion, finely chopped
3 garlic cloves, crushed
1 green chili, chopped
14 ounce can red kidney
   beans, drained
14 ounce can pinto beans, drained

2 tablespoons chopped cilantro
$2/3$ cup vegetable stock
8 wheat tortillas
$1/4$ cup grated vegetarian
   cheddar cheese
salt and pepper

RELISH:
4 scallions, chopped
1 red onion, chopped
1 green chili, chopped
1 tablespoon garlic wine vinegar
1 teaspoon sugar
1 tomato, chopped

1 Heat the oil for the beans in a large skillet. Add the onion and sauté for 3–5 minutes. Add the garlic and chili and cook for 1 minute.

2 Mash the beans with a potato masher and stir into the pan with the cilantro.

3 Stir in the stock and cook the beans, stirring, for 5 minutes, until soft and pulpy.

4 Place the tortillas on a cookie sheet and heat through in a warm oven for about 1–2 minutes.

5 Mix the relish ingredients together.

6 Spoon the beans into a serving dish and top with the cheese. Season well with salt and pepper. Roll the tortillas and serve with the relish and beans.

COOK'S TIP

Add a little more liquid to the beans when they are cooking if they begin to stick to the bottom of the skillet.

Brown Rice, Vegetable, & Herb Gratin

*This is a really filling dish and therefore does not require an accompaniment.
It is very versatile and could be made with a wide selection of vegetables.*

Serves 4

INGREDIENTS

¹/₃ cup brown rice
2 tablespoons butter or margarine
1 red onion, chopped
2 garlic cloves, crushed
1 carrot, cut into matchsticks

1 zucchini, sliced
2³/₄ ounces baby corn cobs,
   halved lengthwise
2 tablespoons sunflower seeds
3 tablespoons chopped mixed herbs

1 cup grated mozzarella cheese
2 tablespoons whole-wheat
   bread crumbs
salt and pepper

1 Cook the rice in a saucepan of boiling salted water for 20 minutes. Drain well.

2 Lightly grease a 3³/₄-cup ovenproof dish.

3 Heat the butter in a skillet. Add the onion and cook, stirring constantly, for 2 minutes, or until softened.

4 Add the garlic, carrot, zucchini, and corn cobs and cook for a further 5 minutes, stirring constantly.

5 Mix the rice with the sunflower seeds and mixed herbs and stir into the pan.

6 Stir in half of the mozzarella cheese and season with salt and pepper to taste.

7 Spoon the mixture into the greased dish and top with the bread crumbs and remaining cheese. Cook in a preheated oven at 350°F for 25–30 minutes, or until the cheese begins to turn golden. Serve at once.

VARIATION

Use an alternative rice, such as basmati, and flavor the dish with curry spices, if desired.

Green Lentil &
Mixed Vegetable Pan-fry

The green lentils used in this recipe require soaking, but are worth it for the flavor.
If time is short, use red split peas which do not require soaking.

Serves 4

INGREDIENTS

$3^3/4$ cups green lentils
4 tablespoons butter or
   vegetarian margarine
2 garlic cloves, crushed
2 tablespoons olive oil
1 tablespoon cider vinegar

1 red onion, cut into eight
$1^3/4$ ounces baby corn cobs,
   halved lengthwise
1 yellow bell pepper, cut into strips
1 red bell pepper, cut into strips
$1^3/4$ ounces green beans, halved

$^1/2$ cup vegetable stock
2 tablespoons honey
salt and pepper
crusty bread, to serve

1 Soak the lentils in a large saucepan of cold water for 25 minutes. Bring to a boil, reduce the heat, and simmer for 20 minutes. Drain thoroughly.

2 Add 1 tablespoon of the butter or margarine, 1 garlic clove, 1 tablespoon of oil, and the vinegar to the lentils and mix well.

3 Melt the remaining butter, and oil in a skillet and stir-fry the garlic, onion, corn cobs, bell peppers and beans for about 3–4 minutes.

4 Add the vegetable stock and bring to a boil. Simmer for 10 minutes, or until the liquid has evaporated.

5 Add the honey and season with salt and pepper to taste. Stir in the lentil mixture and cook for 1 minute to heat through.

Spoon onto warm serving plates and serve with crusty bread.

VARIATION

This pan-fry is very versatile—you can use a mixture of your favorite vegetables, if desired. Try zucchini, carrots, or snow peas.

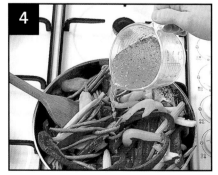

Falafel

These are a very tasty, well-known Middle Eastern dish of small garbanzo bean balls, spiced and deep-fried. They are delicious hot with a crisp tomato salad.

Serves 4

INGREDIENTS

6 cups canned garbanzo
  beans, drained
1 red onion, chopped
3 garlic cloves, crushed
3¹/₂ ounces whole-
  wheat bread
2 small red chilies

1 teaspoon ground cumin
1 teaspoon ground coriander
¹/₂ teaspoon turmeric
1 tablespoon chopped cilantro, plus
  extra to garnish
1 egg, beaten
1 cup whole-wheat bread crumbs

vegetable oil, for deep-frying
salt and pepper
tomato and cucumber salad and
  lemon wedges, to serve

1 Put the garbanzo beans, onion, garlic, bread, chilies, spices, and cilantro in a food processor and process for 30 seconds. Stir and season well.

2 Remove the mixture from the food processor and shape into walnut-size balls.

3 Place the beaten egg in a shallow bowl and place the whole-wheat bread crumbs on a plate. Dip the balls first into the egg to coat and then roll them in the bread crumbs, shaking off any excess.

4 Heat the oil for deep-frying to 350°F or until a cube of bread browns in 30 seconds. Fry the falafel, in batches, for 2–3 minutes, until crisp and browned all over. Remove from the oil with a slotted spoon and drain on absorbent paper towels. Transfer the falafel to a warm serving plate, garnish with cilantro and serve at once with a tomato and cucumber salad and lemon wedges.

COOK'S TIP

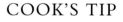

Serve the falafel with a cilantro and yogurt sauce. Thoroughly mix together ²/₃ cup plain yogurt, 2 tablespoons chopped fresh cilantro, and 1 crushed garlic clove.

Cabbage & Walnut Stir-Fry

*This is a really quick, one-pan dish using white
and red cabbage for color and flavor.*

Serves 4

INGREDIENTS

12 ounces white cabbage

12 ounces red cabbage

4 tablespoons peanut oil

1 tablespoon walnut oil

2 garlic cloves, crushed

8 scallions, trimmed

8 ounces firm bean curd, cubed

2 tablespoons lemon juice

1 cup walnut halves

2 teaspoons Dijon mustard

2 teaspoons poppy seeds

salt and pepper

1 Using a sharp knife, shred the white and red cabbages thinly and set aside until required.

2 Heat together the peanut oil and walnut oil in a preheated wok. Add the garlic, cabbage, scallions, and bean curd and cook for 5 minutes, stirring.

3 Add the lemon juice, walnuts, and mustard, season with salt and pepper, and cook for a further 5 minutes, or until the cabbage is tender.

4 Transfer the stir-fry to a warm serving bowl, sprinkle with poppy seeds, and serve.

COOK'S TIP

As well as adding protein, vitamins, and useful fats to the diet, nuts and seeds add flavor and texture to vegetarian meals. Keep a good supply of them in your cupboard, as they can be used in a great variety of dishes—salads, bakes, stir-fries, to name but a few.

VARIATION

Sesame seeds could be used instead of the poppy seeds and drizzle 1 teaspoon of sesame oil over the dish just before serving, if desired.

Spinach Frittata

A frittata is another word for a large, thick omelet. This is an Italian dish which may be made with many flavorings. Spinach is used as the main ingredient in this recipe for color and flavor.

Serves 4

INGREDIENTS

1 pound spinach
2 teaspoons water
4 eggs, beaten
2 tablespoons light cream
2 garlic cloves, crushed

³/4 cup canned corn, drained
1 celery stalk, chopped
1 red chili, chopped
2 tomatoes, seeded and diced
2 tablespoons olive oil
2 tablespoons butter

¹/4 cup pecan nut halves
2 tablespoons grated pecorino cheese
¹/4 cup diced fontina cheese
a pinch of paprika

1 Cook the spinach in 2 teaspoons of water in a covered pan over medium heat for 5 minutes. Drain thoroughly and pat completely dry on absorbent paper towels.

2 Beat the eggs in a bowl and stir in the spinach, light cream, garlic, corn, celery, chili, and tomatoes until the ingredients are well mixed.

3 Heat the oil and butter in an 8-inch heavy-based skillet.

4 Spoon the egg mixture into the skillet and sprinkle with the pecans, pecorino and fontina cheeses, and paprika.

5 Cook without stirring over medium heat for 5–7 minutes, or until the underside of the frittata is brown.

6 Put a large plate over the skillet and invert to turn out the frittata. Slide it back into the skillet and cook the other side for a further 2–3 minutes. Serve the frittata straight from the skillet or transfer to a serving plate.

COOK'S TIP

Be careful not to burn the underside of the frittata during the initial cooking stage—this is why it is important to use a heavy-based skillet. Add a little extra oil to the pan when you turn the frittata over if required.

Marinated Broiled Fennel

Fennel has a wonderful aniseed flavor that makes it ideal for broiling or barbecuing.
Marinated in lime, garlic, oil and mustard, this dish is really delicious.

Serves 4

INGREDIENTS

2 fennel bulbs
1 red bell pepper, cut into large cubes
1 lime, cut into eight wedges

MARINADE:
2 tablespoons lime juice
4 tablespoons olive oil
2 garlic cloves, crushed
1 teaspoon whole-grain mustard
1 tablespoon chopped thyme

fennel fronds, to garnish
crisp salad, to serve

1 Cut each of the fennel bulbs into eight pieces and place in a shallow dish. Mix in the bell peppers.

2 To make the marinade, combine the lime juice, oil, garlic, mustard, and thyme. Pour the marinade over the fennel and bell peppers and set aside to marinate for 1 hour.

3 Thread the fennel and bell peppers onto wooden skewers with the lime wedges.

Preheat a broiler to medium and broil the kebabs for 10 minutes, turning and basting frequently with the marinade.

4 Transfer to serving plates, garnish with fennel fronds and serve with a crisp salad.

VARIATION

Substitute 2 tablespoons orange juice for the lime juice and add 1 tablespoon honey, if desired.

COOK'S TIP

Soak the skewers in water for 20 minutes before using to prevent them from burning during cooking.

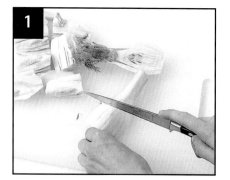

Ciabatta Rolls

Sandwiches are always a welcome snack but can be quite mundane. These crisp ciabatta rolls filled with roast bell peppers and cheese are irresistible and will always be a popular light meal.

Serves 4

INGREDIENTS

4 ciabatta rolls
2 tablespoons olive oil
1 garlic clove crushed

FILLING:
1 red bell pepper
1 green bell pepper
1 yellow bell pepper
4 radishes, sliced
1 bunch watercress
8 tablespoons cream cheese

1 Slice the ciabatta rolls in half. Heat the olive oil and crushed garlic in a saucepan. Pour the oil mixture over the cut surfaces of the rolls and let stand while you prepare the filling.

2 Halve the bell peppers and place, skin side uppermost, on a broiler rack. Cook under a preheated broiler for about 8–10 minutes, until just beginning to char. Remove the bell peppers from the broiler, peel and thinly slice the flesh.

3 Arrange the radish slices on one half of each roll with a few watercress leaves. Spoon the cream cheese on top. Pile the bell peppers on top of the cream cheese and top with the other half of the roll. Serve.

COOK'S TIP

To peel bell peppers, wrap them in foil after broiling. This traps the steam, loosening the skins, and making them easier to peel.

COOK'S TIP

Allow the bell peppers to cool slightly before filling the rolls, otherwise the cheese will melt.

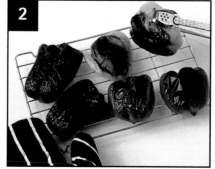

Main Meals

This is the most comprehensive chapter in the book, being perhaps the most important. In a vegetarian diet it is essential to eat a good balance of foods and the following recipes make good use of legumes, grains, bean curd, and vegetables to aid in this quest. The recipes in this chapter will enable you to build a balanced, nutritious, and flavorful menu that will meet all of your needs.

Anyone who ever thought that vegetarian meals were dull will be proved wrong by the rich variety of dishes in this chapter. You'll recognize influences from Indian, Mexican, and Chinese cooking, but there are also traditional stews and casseroles, as well as hearty bakes and roasts. They all make exciting eating at any time of year, on virtually any occasion. There are ideas for midweek meals or for entertaining, some traditional and some more unusual. Don't be afraid to substitute ingredients where appropriate. There is no reason why you cannot enjoy experimenting and adding your own touch to these imaginative ideas.

Mushroom & Spinach Puff Pastry

These puff packets are easy to make and delicious to eat. Filled with garlic,
mushrooms, and spinach, they are ideal with a fresh tomato or cheese sauce.

Serves 4

INGREDIENTS

2 tablespoons butter
1 red onion, halved and sliced
2 garlic cloves, crushed
3 cups button mushrooms, sliced
6 ounces baby spinach

pinch of nutmeg
4 tablespoons heavy cream
8 ounces prepared puff pastry
1 egg, beaten

salt and pepper
2 teaspoons poppy seeds

1 Melt the butter in a skillet. Add the onion and garlic to the pan and sauté for 3–4 minutes, stirring well, until the onion is soft and translucent.

2 Add the mushrooms, spinach, and nutmeg and cook for a further 2–3 minutes.

3 Stir in the heavy cream, mixing well.

4 Season with salt and pepper to taste and remove the skillet from the heat.

5 Roll out the pastry on a lightly floured counter and cut into four 6-inch rounds.

6 Spoon a quarter of the filling onto one half of each round and fold the pastry over to encase the filling. Press down to seal the edges of the pastry and brush with the beaten egg. Sprinkle with the poppy seeds.

7 Place the packets on a dampened cookie sheet and cook in a preheated oven at 400°F for 20 minutes, until cooked

through and the pastry has risen and is golden brown.

8 Transfer the mushroom and spinach puff pastry packets to warm serving plates and serve at once.

COOK'S TIP

The cookie sheet is dampened so that steam forms with the heat of the oven and helps the pastry to rise and set.

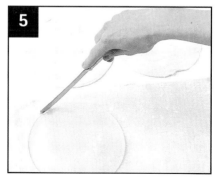

Garbanzo Bean Roast with Sherry Sauce

This is a vegetarian version of the classic "Beef Wellington," and just as delicious.
Served with a sherry sauce and roast vegetables, it makes a tasty and impressive main dish.

Serves 4

INGREDIENTS

1 pound can garbanzo
  beans, drained
1 teaspoon yeast extract
1$^1/_4$ cups chopped walnuts
1$^1/_4$ cups fresh white bread crumbs
1 onion, finely chopped
1$^1/_4$ cups sliced mushrooms
1$^3/_4$ ounces canned corn, drained
2 garlic cloves, crushed
2 tablespoons dry sherry

2 tablespoons vegetable stock
1 tablespoon chopped cilantro
8 ounces prepared puff pastry
1 egg, beaten
2 tablespoons milk
salt and pepper

SAUCE:
1 tablespoon vegetable oil
1 leek, thinly sliced
4 tablespoons dry sherry
$^2/_3$ cup vegetable stock

1 Process the garbanzo beans, yeast extract, nuts, and bread crumbs in a food processor for 30 seconds. In a skillet sauté the onion and mushrooms in their own juices for 3–4 minutes. Stir in the garbanzo bean mixture, corn, and garlic. Add the sherry, stock, cilantro, and seasoning and bind the mixture together. Remove the skillet from the heat and set aside to cool completely.

2 Roll out the pastry on a lightly floured counter to form a rectangle 14 inches x 12 inches. Shape the garbanzo bean mixture into a loaf shape and wrap the pastry around it, sealing the edges. Place seam side down on a dampened cookie sheet and score the top in a criss-cross pattern. Mix the egg and milk and brush over the pastry. Cook in a preheated oven at 400°F for 25–30 minutes. Heat the oil for the sauce in a pan and sauté the leek for 5 minutes. Add the sherry and stock and bring to a boil. Simmer for 5 minutes and serve with the roast.

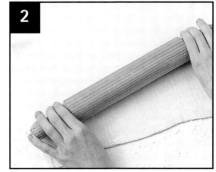

Kidney Bean Kiev

This is a vegetarian version of chicken kiev, the bean patties taking the place of the chicken. Topped with garlic and herb butter and coated in bread crumbs, this version is just as delicious.

Serves 4

INGREDIENTS

GARLIC BUTTER:
8 tablespoons butter
3 garlic cloves, crushed
1 tablespoon chopped parsley

BEAN PATTIES:
1 pound 7 ounces canned red
  kidney beans
1¼ cups fresh white bread crumbs
2 tablespoons butter
1 leek, chopped

1 celery stalk, chopped
1 tablespoon chopped parsley
1 egg, beaten
salt and pepper
vegetable oil, for shallow frying

1 To make the garlic butter, put the butter, garlic, and parsley in a bowl and blend together with a wooden spoon. Place the garlic butter mixture on a sheet of waxed paper, roll into a cigar shape, and wrap in the baking parchment. Chill in the refrigerator until required.

2 Using a potato masher, mash the red kidney beans in a mixing bowl and stir in ¾ cup of the bread crumbs until the mixture is thoroughly blended.

3 Melt the butter in a skillet and sauté the leek and celery for 3–4 minutes, stirring.

4 Add the bean mixture to the skillet, together with the parsley, season with salt and pepper to taste and mix well. Remove from the heat and let cool slightly.

5 Shape the bean mixture into 4 equal-size ovals.

6 Slice the garlic butter into 4 and place a slice in the center of each bean patty. Mold the bean mixture around the garlic butter to encase it completely.

7 Dip each bean patty first into the beaten egg to coat and then roll them in the remaining bread crumbs.

8 Heat a little oil in a skillet and fry the patties, turning once, for 7–10 minutes, or until golden. Serve at once.

Cashew Paella

Paella traditionally contains chicken and fish, but this recipe is packed with vegetables and nuts for a truly delicious and simple vegetarian dish.

Serves 4

INGREDIENTS

2 tablespoons olive oil
1 tablespoon butter
1 red onion, chopped
1 cup risotto rice
1 teaspoon ground turmeric
1 teaspoon ground cumin
$^1/_2$ teaspoon chili powder
3 garlic cloves, crushed
1 green chili, sliced

1 green bell pepper, diced
1 red bell pepper, diced
$2^3/_4$ ounces baby corn,
   halved lengthwise
2 tablespoons pitted black olives
1 large tomato, seeded and diced
2 cups vegetable stock

$^3/_4$ cup unsalted cashews
$^1/_4$ cup frozen peas
2 tablespoons chopped parsley
pinch of cayenne pepper
salt and pepper
fresh herbs, to garnish

1 Heat together the olive oil and butter in a large, heavy-based skillet or paella pan until the butter has melted.

2 Add the chopped onion to the skillet and sauté for 2–3 minutes, stirring, until the onion has softened.

3 Stir in the rice, turmeric, cumin, chili powder, garlic, chili, bell peppers, corn cobs, olives, and tomato and cook over medium heat for 1–2 minutes, stirring occasionally.

4 Pour in the stock and bring the mixture to a boil. Reduce the heat and cook for 20 minutes, stirring constantly.

5 Add the cashew nuts and peas to the mixture in the skillet and cook for a further 5 minutes, stirring occasionally. Season to taste with salt and pepper and sprinkle with parsley and cayenne pepper. Transfer to warm serving plates, garnish, and serve at once.

COOK'S TIP

For authenticity and flavor, use a few saffron strands soaked in a little boiling water instead of the turmeric. Saffron has a lovely, nutty flavor.

Vegetable & Bean Curd Strudels

*These strudels look really impressive and are perfect if friends are coming
to visit or for a more formal dinner party dish.*

Serves 4

INGREDIENTS

FILLING:
2 tablespoons vegetable oil
2 tablespoons butter or vegetarian
  margarine
$^1/_3$ cup finely diced potatoes
1 leek, shredded
2 garlic cloves, crushed

1 teaspoon garam masala
$^1/_2$ teaspoon chili powder
$^1/_2$ teaspoon turmeric
$1^3/_4$ ounces okra, sliced
$1^1/_4$ cups sliced button mushrooms,
2 tomatoes, diced
8 ounces firm bean curd, diced

12 sheets phyllo pastry
2 tablespoons butter or vegetarian
  margarine, melted
salt and pepper

1 To make the filling, heat the
oil and butter in a skillet. Add
the potatoes and leek and cook for
2–3 minutes, stirring.

2 Add the garlic and spices,
okra, mushrooms, tomatoes,
bean curd, and seasoning and
cook, stirring, for 5–7 minutes, or
until tender.

3 Lay the pastry out on a
chopping board and brush
each individual sheet with butter.

Place 3 sheets on top of one
another. Repeat to make 4 stacks.

4 Spoon a quarter of the filling
along the center of each stack
and brush the edges with butter.
Fold the short edges in and roll up
lengthwise to form a cigar shape;
and brush the outside with butter.
Place the strudels on a greased
cookie sheet.

5 Cook in a preheated oven at
375°F and cook the strudels

for 20 minutes or until golden
brown. Serve at once.

COOK'S TIP

*Decorate the outside of the
strudels with crumpled pastry
trimmings before cooking for a
really impressive effect.*

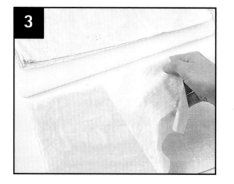

Vegetable Lasagne

This colorful and tasty lasagne, with layers of vegetables in tomato sauce and eggplant, all topped with a rich cheese sauce is simply delicious.

Serves 4

INGREDIENTS

1 eggplant, sliced
3 tablespoons olive oil
2 garlic cloves, crushed
1 red onion, halved and sliced
1 green bell pepper, diced
1 red bell pepper, diced
1 yellow bell pepper, diced
3 cups sliced mixed mushrooms,
2 celery stalks, sliced
1 zucchini, diced
$^1/_2$ teaspoon chili powder

$^1/_2$ teaspoon ground cumin
2 tomatoes, chopped
1$^1/_4$ cups sieved tomatoes
2 tablespoons chopped basil
8 lasagne noodles
salt and pepper

CHEESE SAUCE:
2 tablespoons butter or
  vegetarian margarine
1 tablespoon flour
$^2/_3$ cup vegetable stock
1$^1/_4$ cups milk
$^3/_4$ cup grated vegetarian
  Cheddar cheese
1 teaspoon Dijon mustard
1 tablespoon chopped basil
1 egg, beaten

1 Place the eggplant slices in a colander, sprinkle with salt, and set aside for 20 minutes. Rinse under cold water, drain, and reserve. Heat the oil in a pan and sauté the garlic and onion for 1–2 minutes. Add the bell peppers, mushrooms, celery, and zucchini and cook for about 3–4 minutes, stirring. Stir in the spices and cook for 1 minute. Mix the tomatoes, sieved tomatoes, and basil together and season well.

2 For the sauce, melt the butter in a pan, add the flour, and cook, stirring constantly, for 1 minute. Remove from the heat and stir in the stock and milk. Return to the heat and add half of the cheese and the mustard. Boil, stirring, until thickened. Stir in the basil and season to taste with salt and pepper. Remove from the heat and stir in the egg. Place half of the lasagne noodles in an ovenproof dish. Top with half of the vegetables, then half of the tomato sauce. Cover with half the eggplants. Repeat and spoon the cheese sauce on top. Sprinkle with cheese and cook in a preheated oven at 350°F for 40 minutes.

Lentil & Rice Casserole

This is a really hearty dish, perfect for cold days
when a filling hot dish is just what you need.

Serves 4

INGREDIENTS

1¼ cups red split lentils
⅓ cup long-grain white rice
5 cups vegetable stock
⅔ cup dry white wine
1 leek, cut into chunks
3 garlic cloves, crushed
14 ounce can chopped tomatoes
1 teaspoon ground cumin
1 teaspoon chili powder

1 teaspoon garam masala
1 red bell pepper, sliced
3½ ounces small broccoli florets
8 baby corn, halved lengthwise
1¾ ounces green beans, halved
1 tablespoon fresh basil, shredded
salt and pepper
fresh basil sprigs, to garnish

1 Place the lentils, rice, vegetable stock, and white wine in a flameproof casserole, bring to a boil, and simmer over gentle heat for about 20 minutes, stirring occasionally.

2 Add the leek, garlic, tomatoes, cumin, chili powder, garam masala, bell pepper, broccoli, baby corn, and green beans.

3 Bring the mixture to a boil, reduce the heat, cover the casserole, and simmer for a further 10–15 minutes, or until the vegetables are tender.

4 Add the shredded basil and season with salt and pepper to taste.

5 Garnish with fresh basil sprigs and serve at once.

VARIATION

You can vary the rice in this recipe—use brown or wild rice, if desired.

Vegetable Hot Pot

*In this recipe, a variety of vegetables are cooked under a layer of potatoes,
topped with cheese, and cooked until golden brown for a filling and tasty meal.*

Serves 4

INGREDIENTS

2 large potatoes, thinly sliced
2 tablespoons vegetable oil
1 red onion, halved and sliced
1 leek, sliced
2 garlic cloves, crushed
1 carrot, cut into chunks
3^1/$_2$ ounces broccoli florets

3^1/$_2$ ounces cauliflower florets
2 small turnips, quartered
1 tablespoon all-purpose flour
3^1/$_2$ cups vegetable stock
^{2}/$_3$ cup hard cider
1 eating apple, sliced
2 tablespoons chopped sage

pinch of cayenne pepper
^{1}/$_2$ cup grated vegetarian
   Cheddar cheese
salt and pepper

1 Cook the potato slices in a saucepan of boiling water for 10 minutes. Drain thoroughly and reserve.

2 Heat the oil in a flameproof casserole dish and sauté the onion, leek, and garlic for 2–3 minutes. Add the remaining vegetables and cook for a further 3–4 minutes, stirring.

3 Stir in the flour and cook for 1 minute. Gradually add the stock and cider and bring the mixture to a boil. Add the apple, sage, and cayenne pepper and season well. Remove the dish from the heat. Transfer the vegetables to an ovenproof dish.

4 Arrange the potato slices on top of the vegetable mixture to cover.

5 Sprinkle the cheese on top of the potato slices and cook in a preheated oven at 375°F for 30–35 minutes or until the potato is golden brown and beginning to crispen slightly around the edges. Serve at once.

COOK'S TIP

If the potato begins to brown too quickly, cover with foil for the last 10 minutes of cooking time to prevent the top from burning.

Vegetable Chop Suey

*A classic Chinese dish found on all restaurant menus,
this recipe is quick to prepare and makes a tasty meal.*

Serves 4

INGREDIENTS

2 tablespoons peanut oil
1 onion, chopped
3 garlic cloves, chopped
1 green bell pepper, diced
1 red bell pepper, diced
2³/₄ ounces broccoli florets

1 zucchini, sliced
1 ounce green beans
1 carrot, cut into matchsticks
3¹/₂ ounces bean sprouts
2 teaspoons light brown sugar
2 tablespoons light soy sauce

¹/₂ cup vegetable stock
salt and pepper
noodles, to serve

1 Heat the oil in a preheated wok until almost smoking. Add the onion and garlic and stir-fry for 30 seconds.

2 Stir in the bell peppers, broccoli, zucchini, beans, and carrot and stir-fry for a further 2–3 minutes.

3 Add the bean sprouts, light brown sugar, soy sauce, and vegetable stock. Season with salt and pepper to taste and cook for about 2 minutes.

4 Transfer the vegetables to serving plates and serve at once with noodles.

COOK'S TIP

The clever design of a wok, with its spherical base and high sloping sides, enables the food to be tossed so that it is cooked quickly and evenly. It is essential to heat the wok sufficiently before you add the ingredients to ensure quick and even cooking.

COOK'S TIP

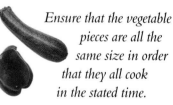

Ensure that the vegetable pieces are all the same size in order that they all cook in the stated time.

VARIATION

Add 1 tablespoon chili oil for a hotter flavor and add cashew nuts for extra crunch.

Vegetable Toad-in-the-Hole

This dish can be made in one large dish or in individual Yorkshire pudding pans.

Serves 4

INGREDIENTS

BATTER:
³/₄ cup all-purpose flour
2 eggs, beaten
³/₄ cup milk
2 tablespoons whole-grain mustard
2 tablespoons vegetable oil

FILLING:
2 tablespoons butter
2 garlic cloves, crushed
1 onion, cut into eight
2³/₄ ounces baby carrots, halved
   lengthwise
1³/₄ ounces green beans

1³/₄ ounces canned corn, drained
2 tomatoes, seeded and cut
   into chunks
1 teaspoon whole-grain mustard
1 tablespoon chopped mixed herbs
salt and pepper

1 To make the batter, sift the flour and a pinch of salt into a large bowl. Make a well in the center and beat in the eggs and milk to make a batter. Stir in the mustard and let stand.

2 Pour the oil into a shallow ovenproof dish and heat in a preheated oven at 400°F for 10 minutes.

3 To make the filling, melt the butter in a skillet and sauté the garlic and onion for 2 minutes, stirring. Cook the carrots and beans in a saucepan of boiling water for 7 minutes, or until tender. Drain well.

4 Add the corn and tomato to the skillet, together with the mustard and herbs. Season well with salt and pepper and add the carrots and beans.

5 Remove the dish from the oven and pour in the batter.

Spoon the vegetables into the center, return to the oven and cook for 30–35 minutes, until the batter has risen and set. Serve the vegetable toad-in-the-hole at once.

COOK'S TIP

It is important that the oil is hot before adding the batter, so that the batter begins to cook and rise at once.

Vegetable Jalousie

This is a really easy dish to make, but looks impressive.
The mixture of vegetables gives the dish a wonderful color and flavor.

Serves 4

INGREDIENTS

1 pound prepared puff pastry	1 leek, shredded	2 tablespoons all-purpose flour
1 egg, beaten	2 garlic cloves, crushed	6 tablespoons vegetable stock
	1 red bell pepper, sliced	6 tablespoons milk
FILLING:	1 yellow bell pepper, sliced	4 tablespoons dry white wine
2 tablespoons butter or	$^3/_4$ cup sliced mushrooms	1 tablespoon chopped oregano
vegetarian margarine	$2^3/_4$ ounces small asparagus spears	salt and pepper

1 Melt the butter or margarine in a skillet and sauté the leek and garlic for 2 minutes, stirring. Add the remaining vegetables and cook, stirring, for 3–4 minutes.

2 Add the flour and cook, stirring, for 1 minute. Remove the skillet from the heat and stir in the vegetable stock, milk, and white wine. Return the skillet to the heat and bring to a boil, stirring, until thickened. Stir in the oregano and season with salt and pepper to taste.

3 Roll half of the pastry out on a lightly floured counter to form a rectangle 15 inches x 6 inches.

4 Roll out the other half of the pastry to the same shape, but a little larger. Put the smaller rectangle on a cookie sheet lined with dampened baking parchment.

5 Spoon the filling evenly over the top of the smaller pastry rectangle, leaving a ½-inch clean edge.

6 Cut parallel slits across the larger rectangle at a slight angle to within 1 inch of each edge.

7 Brush the edge of the smaller rectangle with egg and place the larger rectangle on top, sealing the edges well.

8 Brush the whole jalousie with egg to glaze and cook in a preheated oven at 400°F for 30–35 minutes, until risen and golden. Serve at once.

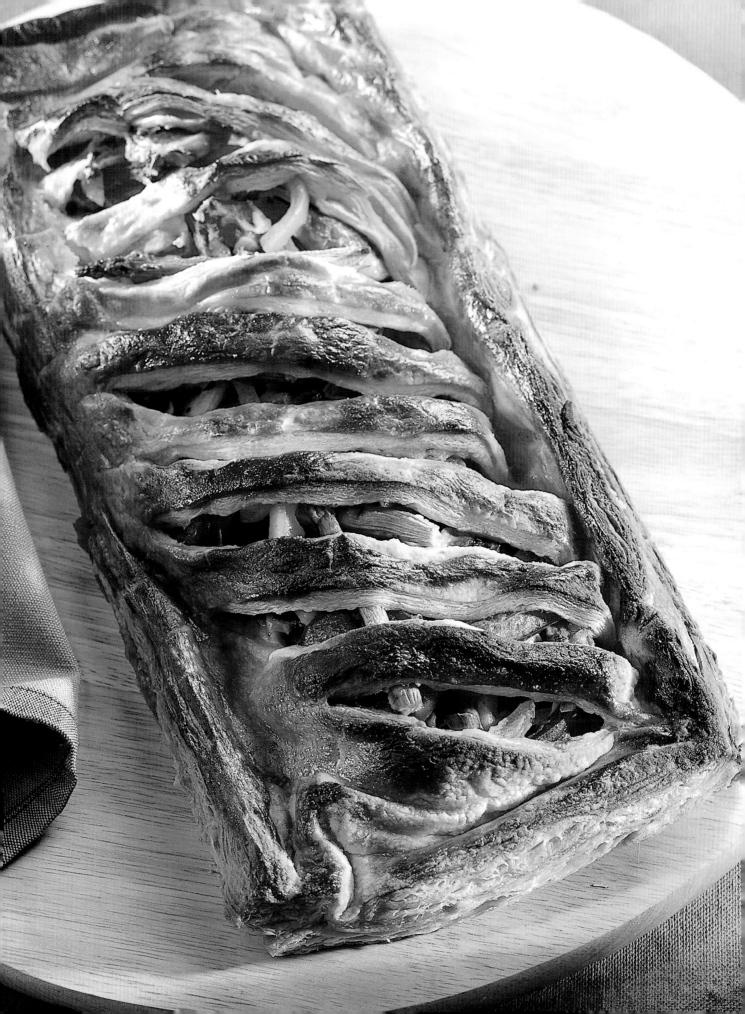

Cauliflower, Broccoli, & Cheese Flan

*This really is a tasty flan, the pastry case for which may
be made in advance and frozen until required.*

Serves 8

INGREDIENTS

PASTRY:
1¼ cups all-purpose flour
pinch of salt
½ teaspoon paprika
1 teaspoon dried thyme
6 tablespoons vegetarian margarine
3 tablespoons water

FILLING:
3½ ounces cauliflower florets
3½ ounces broccoli florets
1 onion, cut into eight
2 tablespoons butter or
  vegetarian margarine
1 tablespoon all-purpose flour
6 tablespoons vegetable stock

8 tablespoons milk
¾ cup grated vegetarian
  Cheddar cheese
salt and pepper
paprika and thyme, to garnish

1 To make the pastry, sift the flour and salt into a bowl. Add the paprika and thyme and rub in the margarine. Stir in the water and bind to form a dough.

2 Roll out the pastry on a floured counter and use to line a 7-inch loose-based flan pan. Prick the base with a fork and line with baking parchment. Fill with ceramic baking beans and bake in a preheated oven at 375°F for 15 minutes. Remove the parchment and beans and return the pastry case to the oven for a further 5 minutes.

3 To make the filling, cook the vegetables in a pan of boiling water for 10–12 minutes, until tender. Drain and reserve.

4 Melt the butter in a pan. Add the flour and cook, stirring, for 1 minute. Remove from the heat, stir in the stock and milk, and return to the heat. Bring to a boil, stirring, and add ½ cup of the grated cheese. Season to taste with salt and pepper.

5 Spoon the cauliflower, broccoli, and onion into the pastry case. Pour in the sauce and sprinkle with the cheese. Return to the oven for 10 minutes, until the cheese is bubbling. Dust with paprika, garnish and serve.

Roast Bell Pepper Tart

This tastes truly delicious, the flavor of roasted vegetables being entirely different from that of boiled or fried.

Serves 8

INGREDIENTS

PASTRY:
1 1/4 cups all-purpose flour
pinch of salt
6 tablespoons butter or
    vegetarian margarine
2 tablespoons green pitted olives,
    finely chopped
3 tablespoons cold water

FILLING:
1 red bell pepper
1 green bell pepper
1 yellow bell pepper
2 garlic cloves, crushed
2 tablespoons olive oil
1 cup grated mozzarella cheese
2 eggs

2/3 cup milk
1 tablespoon chopped basil
salt and pepper

1 To make the pastry, sift the flour and a pinch of salt into a bowl. Rub in the butter or margarine until the mixture resembles bread crumbs. Add the olives and cold water, bringing the mixture together to form a dough.

2 Roll out the dough on a floured counter and use to line an 8-inch based flan pan. Prick the base with a fork and chill in the refrigerator.

3 Cut the bell peppers in half lengthwise and arrange in a single layer skin side uppermost on a cookie sheet. Mix the garlic and oil and brush over the bell peppers. Cook in a preheated oven at 400°F for 20 minutes, or until they are beginning to blister and char slightly. Let the bell peppers cool slightly and thinly slice. Arrange in the base of the pastry case, layering with the grated mozzarella cheese.

4 Beat the egg and milk and add the basil. Season and pour over the bell peppers. Put the tart on a cookie sheet and return to the oven for 20 minutes, or until set. Serve hot or cold.

COOK'S TIP

Make sure that the olives are very finely chopped, otherwise they will make holes in the pastry.

Vegetable Biryani

The Biryani originated in the North of India, and was a dish reserved for festivals. The vegetables are marinated in a yogurt-based marinade and cooked in a casserole with the rice and onions.

Serves 4

INGREDIENTS

1 large potato, cubed
3$^{1}/_{2}$ ounces baby carrots
1$^{3}/_{4}$ ounces okra, thickly sliced
2 celery stalks, sliced
2$^{3}/_{4}$ ounces baby button
   mushrooms, halved

1 eggplant, halved and sliced
1$^{1}/_{4}$ cups plain yogurt
1 tablespoon grated root ginger
2 large onions, grated
4 garlic cloves, crushed
1 teaspoon turmeric
1 tablespoon curry powder

2 tablespoons butter
2 onions, sliced
1$^{1}/_{4}$ cups basmati rice
chopped cilantro, to garnish

1 Cook the potato cubes, carrots, and okra in a pan of boiling salted water for 7–8 minutes. Drain well and place in a large bowl. Mix with the celery, mushrooms, and eggplant.

2 Mix together the plain yogurt, ginger, grated onions, garlic, turmeric, and curry powder and spoon over the vegetables, tossing to coat thoroughly. Set aside to marinate for at least 2 hours.

3 Heat the butter in a skillet and cook the sliced onions for 5–6 minutes, until golden brown. Remove a few onions from the skillet and reserve for garnishing.

4 Cook the rice in a pan of boiling water for 7 minutes. Drain well.

5 Add the marinated vegetables to the onions in the skillet and cook, stirring occasionally, for 10 minutes.

6 Put half of the rice in a 9-cup casserole dish. Spoon the vegetables on top and cover with the remaining rice. Cover and cook in a preheated oven at 375°F for 20–25 minutes, or until the rice is tender.

7 Spoon the vegetable biryani onto a warm serving plate, garnish with the reserved fried onions and chopped cilantro, and serve at once.

Baked Cheese & Tomato Macaroni

*This is a really simple, family dish which is easy
to prepare and cook. Serve with a salad.*

Serves 4

INGREDIENTS

2 cups elbow macaroni
1¹/₂ cups grated vegetarian cheese
1 cup grated Parmesan cheese
4 tablespoons fresh white
 bread crumbs
1 tablespoon chopped basil

1 tablespoon butter or margarine

TOMATO SAUCE:
1 tablespoon olive oil
1 shallot, finely chopped
2 garlic cloves, crushed

1 pound canned chopped tomatoes
1 tablespoon chopped basil
salt and pepper

1 To make the tomato sauce, heat the oil in a saucepan and sauté the shallots and garlic for 1 minute. Add the tomatoes and basil, and salt and pepper to taste, and cook over a medium heat, stirring, for 10 minutes.

2 Meanwhile, cook the macaroni in a pan of boiling salted water for 8 minutes, or until almost tender. Drain.

3 Mix both of the cheeses together.

4 Grease a deep, ovenproof dish. Spoon a third of the tomato sauce into the base of the dish, top with a third of the macaroni, and then a third of the cheeses. Season with salt and pepper. Repeat the layers twice.

5 Combine the bread crumbs and basil and sprinkle over the top. Dot with the butter or margarine and cook in a preheated oven at 375°F for 25 minutes, or until the dish is golden brown and bubbling. Serve at once.

COOK'S TIP

*Use other pasta
shapes, such as
penne, if you have
them at hand, instead
of the macaroni.*

Garbanzo Bean & Vegetable Casserole

This hearty dish is best served with warm crusty bread to sop up the delicious juices.

Serves 4

INGREDIENTS

1 tablespoon olive oil
1 red onion, halved and sliced
3 garlic cloves, crushed
8 ounces spinach
1 fennel bulb, cut into eight
1 red bell pepper, diced

1 tablespoon all-purpose flour
$3^3/_4$ cups vegetable stock
6 tablespoons dry white wine
14 ounce can garbanzo
 beans, drained
1 bay leaf

1 teaspoon ground coriander
$^1/_2$ teaspoons paprika
salt and pepper
fennel fronds, to garnish

1 Heat the olive oil in a large flameproof casserole and sauté the onion and garlic for 1 minute, stirring. Add the spinach and cook for 4 minutes, or until wilted.

2 Add the fennel and bell pepper and cook for 2 minutes, stirring.

3 Stir in the flour and cook, stirring, for 1 minute.

4 Add the stock, wine, garbanzo beans, bay leaf, coriander, and paprika, cover, and cook for 30 minutes. Season to taste, garnish with fennel fronds and serve at once.

VARIATION

Replace the coriander with nutmeg, if desired, as it works particularly well with spinach.

COOK'S TIP

Use other canned varieties or mixed beans instead of the garbanzo beans, if desired.

Sweet & Sour Vegetables & Bean Curd

Serve this dish with plain noodles or fluffy white rice for a filling, Chinese-style meal.

Serves 4

INGREDIENTS

1 tablespoon peanut oil
2 garlic cloves, crushed
1 teaspoon grated ginger root
1³/₄ ounces baby corn
1³/₄ ounces snow peas
1 carrot, cut into matchsticks

1 green bell pepper, cut into matchsticks
8 scallions, trimmed
1³/₄ ounces canned bamboo shoots
8 ounces marinated firm bean curd, cubed
2 tablespoons dry sherry

2 tablespoons rice vinegar
2 tablespoons honey
1 tablespoon light soy sauce
²/₃ cup vegetable stock
1 tablespoon cornstarch

1 Heat the oil in a preheated wok until almost smoking.

2 Add the garlic and grated ginger root and cook for 30 seconds, stirring frequently.

3 Add the baby corn, snow peas, carrot, and bell pepper and stir-fry for about 5 minutes or until the vegetables are tender.

4 Add the scallions, bamboo shoots, and bean curd and cook for a further 2 minutes.

5 Stir in the sherry, rice vinegar, honey, soy sauce, vegetable stock, and cornstarch and bring to a boil. Reduce the heat and simmer for 2 minutes. Transfer to serving dishes and serve at once.

VARIATION

You can replace any of the vegetables in this dish with others of your choice. For a colorful, attractive stir-fry, select vegetables with bright, contrasting colors.

Spicy Potato & Lemon Casserole

*This is based on a Moroccan dish in which potatoes are spiced
with cilantro and cumin and cooked in a lemon sauce.*

Serves 4

INGREDIENTS

1/2 cup olive oil

2 red onions, cut into eight

3 garlic cloves, crushed

2 teaspoons ground cumin

2 teaspoons ground coriander

pinch of cayenne pepper

1 carrot, thickly sliced

2 small turnips, quartered

1 zucchini, sliced

1 pound potatoes, thickly sliced

juice and rind of 2 large lemons

1 1/4 cups vegetable stock

2 tablespoons chopped cilantro

salt and pepper

1 Heat the olive oil in a flameproof casserole.

2 Add the red onion and sauté for 3 minutes, stirring.

3 Add the garlic and cook for 30 seconds. Mix in the spices and cook for 1 minute, stirring.

4 Add the carrot, turnips, zucchini, and potatoes and stir to coat in the oil.

5 Add the lemon juice, rind, stock, and salt and pepper to taste, cover, and cook over medium heat for 20–30 minutes, stirring occasionally.

6 Remove the lid, sprinkle in the cilantro, and stir well. Serve at once.

COOK'S TIP

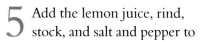

A selection of spices and herbs is important for adding variety to your cooking—add to your range each time you try a new recipe.

COOK'S TIP

Check the vegetables while cooking as they may begin to stick to the pan. Add a little more boiling water or stock if necessary.

Vegetable Cannelloni

*This dish is made with prepared cannelloni tubes,
but may also be made by rolling ready-made lasagne sheets.*

Serves 4

INGREDIENTS

1 eggplant
$1/2$ cup olive oil
8 ounces spinach
2 garlic cloves, crushed
1 teaspoon ground cumin
1 cup chopped mushrooms
12 cannelloni tubes

salt and pepper

TOMATO SAUCE:
1 tablespoon olive oil
1 onion, chopped
2 garlic cloves, crushed
2 x 14 ounce cans chopped tomatoes

1 teaspoon superfine sugar
2 tablespoons chopped basil
$1/2$ cup sliced mozzarella

1 With a sharp knife, cut the eggplant into small dice.

2 Heat the oil in a skillet and cook the eggplant for 2–3 minutes.

3 Add the spinach, garlic, cumin, and mushrooms. Season and cook for 2–3 minutes, stirring. Spoon the mixture into the cannelloni tubes and arrange them in an ovenproof dish in a single layer.

4 To make the sauce, heat the olive oil in a saucepan and sauté the onion and garlic for 1 minute. Add the tomatoes, superfine sugar, and chopped basil and bring to a boil. Reduce the heat and simmer for about 5 minutes. Pour the sauce over the cannelloni tubes.

5 Arrange the sliced mozzarella on top of the sauce and cook in a preheated oven at 375°F for 30 minutes, or until the cheese is bubbling and golden brown. Serve at once straight from the dish.

COOK'S TIP

*You can prepare the
tomato sauce in advance and
store it in the refrigerator
for up to 24 hours.*

Cauliflower Bake

The red of the tomatoes is a great contrast to the cauliflower and herbs,
making this dish appealing to both the eye and the palate.

Serves 4

INGREDIENTS

1 pound cauliflower, broken
  into florets
2 large potatoes, cubed
3 1/2 ounces cherry tomatoes

SAUCE:
2 tablespoons butter or
  vegetarian margarine
1 leek, sliced
1 garlic clove, crushed
3 tablespoons all-purpose flour
1 1/4 cups milk

3/4 cup mixed grated cheese,
  such as vegetarian cheddar,
  parmesan, and swiss cheese
1/2 teaspoon paprika
2 tablespoons chopped flat
  leaf parsley
salt and pepper
chopped fresh parsley, to garnish

1 Cook the cauliflower in a saucepan of boiling water for 10 minutes. Drain well and reserve. Meanwhile, cook the potatoes in a pan of boiling water for 10 minutes, drain, and reserve.

2 To make the sauce, melt the butter or margarine in a saucepan and sauté the leek and garlic for 1 minute. Add the flour and cook, stirring constantly, for 1 minute. Remove the pan from the heat and gradually stir in the milk, 1/2 cup of the grated cheese, the paprika, and parsley. Return the pan to the heat and bring to a boil, stirring constantly. Season with salt and pepper to taste.

3 Spoon the cauliflower into a deep ovenproof dish. Add the cherry tomatoes and top with the potatoes. Pour the sauce over the potatoes and sprinkle on the remaining cheese.

4 Cook in a preheated oven at 350°F for 20 minutes, or until the vegetables are cooked through and the cheese is golden brown and bubbling. Garnish with parsley and serve at once.

VARIATION

This dish could also be made with broccoli instead of cauliflower.

Leek & Herb Soufflé

Hot soufflés look very impressive if served as soon as they
come out of the oven, otherwise they will sink quite quickly.

Serves 4

INGREDIENTS

12 ounces baby leeks
1 tablespoon olive oil
$^{1}/_{2}$ cup vegetable stock

$^{1}/_{2}$ cup walnuts
2 eggs, separated
2 tablespoons chopped mixed herbs

2 tablespoons plain yogurt
salt and pepper

1 Using a sharp knife, chop the leeks finely.

2 Heat the oil in a skillet and sauté the leeks, stirring, for 2–3 minutes.

3 Add the stock to the skillet and cook over gentle heat for a further 5 minutes.

4 Place the walnuts in a food processor and process until finely chopped.

5 Add the leek mixture to the nuts and process to form a purée. Transfer to a mixing bowl.

6 Combine the egg yolks, herbs, and yogurt and pour into the leek purée. Season with salt and pepper to taste and mix thoroughly.

7 In a separate mixing bowl, whisk the egg whites until firm peaks form.

8 Fold the egg whites into the leek mixture. Spoon the mixture into a lightly greased 3¾-cup soufflé dish and place on a warmed cookie sheet.

9 Cook in a preheated oven at 350°F for 35–40 minutes, or

until just set and the top is golden brown. Serve the soufflé at once.

COOK'S TIP

Placing the soufflé dish
on a warm cookie sheet helps to
cook the soufflé from the bottom,
thus aiding its cooking, so that it is
light and airy.

Artichoke & Cheese Tart

Artichoke hearts are delicious to eat, being very delicate in flavor and appearance.
They are ideal for cooking in a cheese-flavored pastry case.

Serves 8

INGREDIENTS

1¼ cups whole wheat flour
2 garlic cloves, crushed
6 tablespoons butter or
   vegetarian margarine
salt and pepper

FILLING:
2 tablespoons olive oil
1 red onion, halved and sliced
10 canned or fresh artichoke hearts
1 cup grated vegetarian
   Cheddar cheese

½ cup crumbled gorgonzola cheese
2 eggs, beaten
1 tablespoon chopped fresh rosemary
⅔ cup milk

1 Make the pastry. Sift the flour into a bowl, add a pinch of salt and the garlic. Rub in the butter or margarine until the mixture resembles bread crumbs. Stir in 3 tablespoons of water and mix to form a dough.

2 Roll out the pastry on a lightly floured counter to fit an 8-inch pie pan. Prick the pastry with a fork.

3 Heat the oil in a skillet and sauté the onion, stirring, for 3 minutes. Add the artichoke hearts and cook for a further 2 minutes.

4 Mix the cheeses with the beaten eggs, rosemary, and milk. Stir in the drained artichoke mixture and season to taste.

5 Spoon the artichoke and cheese mixture into the pastry case and cook in a preheated oven at 400°F for 25 minutes, or until cooked and set. Serve the quiche hot or cold.

COOK'S TIP

Gently press the center of the quiche with your fingertip to test if it is cooked through. It should feel fairly firm, but not solid. If overcooked the quiche will begin to "weep."

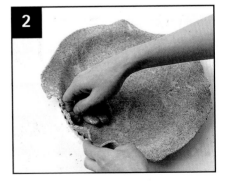

Tagliatelle with Zucchini Sauce

*This is a really fresh tasting dish which is ideal with
a crisp white wine and some crusty bread.*

Serves 4

INGREDIENTS

1 pound 7 ounces zucchini
6 tablespoons olive oil
3 garlic cloves, crushed
3 tablespoons chopped basil
2 red chilies, sliced

juice of 1 large lemon
5 tablespoons light cream
4 tablespoons freshly grated
  Parmesan cheese
8 ounces tagliatelle

salt and pepper
salad greens and grated Parmesan
  cheese, to serve (optional)

1 Using a vegetable peeler, slice the zucchini into very thin ribbons.

2 Heat the oil in a skillet and sauté the garlic for about 30 seconds.

3 Add the zucchini and cook over gentle heat, stirring, for 5–7 minutes.

4 Stir in the basil, chilies, lemon juice, light cream, and grated Parmesan cheese and season with salt and pepper to taste.

5 Meanwhile, cook the tagliatelle in a large pan of lightly salted boiling water for 10 minutes, until "al dente." Drain the pasta thoroughly and transfer to a warm serving bowl.

6 Pile the zucchini mixture on top of the pasta. Serve at once with salad greens and extra Parmesan, if desired.

VARIATION

Lime juice and zest could be used instead of the lemon as an alternative.

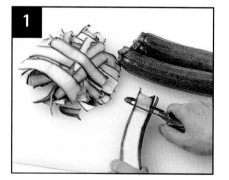

Olive, Bell Pepper, & Cherry Tomato Pasta

The sweet cherry tomatoes in this recipe add color and flavor and are complemented by the black olives and bell peppers.

Serves 4

INGREDIENTS

2 cups penne
2 tablespoons olive oil
2 tablespoons butter
2 garlic cloves, crushed
1 green bell pepper, thinly sliced

1 yellow bell pepper, thinly sliced
16 cherry tomatoes, halved
1 tablespoon chopped oregano
$1/2$ cup dry white wine

2 tablespoons quartered, pitted
   black olives
$2^3/4$ ounces arugula
salt and pepper
fresh oregano sprigs, to garnish

1 Cook the pasta in a saucepan of boiling salted water for 8–10 minutes, or until "al dente." Drain thoroughly.

2 Heat the oil and butter in a pan until the butter melts. Sauté the garlic for 30 seconds. Add the bell peppers and cook for 3–4 minutes, stirring.

3 Stir in the cherry tomatoes, oregano, wine, and olives and cook for 3–4 minutes. Season well with salt and pepper and stir in the arugula until just wilted.

4 Transfer the pasta to a serving dish, spoon over the sauce, and mix well. Garnish and serve.

VARIATION

If arugula is unavailable, spinach makes a good substitute. Follow the same cooking instructions as for arugula.

COOK'S TIP

Ensure that the saucepan is large enough to prevent the pasta from sticking together during cooking.

Spinach & Pine Nut Pasta

*Use any pasta shapes that you have for this recipe,
the tricolore pasta being visually the best to use.*

Serves 4

INGREDIENTS

8 ounces pasta shapes or spaghetti
$^{1}/_{2}$ cup olive oil
2 garlic cloves, crushed
1 onion, quartered and sliced
3 large flat mushrooms, sliced

8 ounces spinach
2 tablespoons pine nuts
6 tablespoons dry white wine
salt and pepper
Parmesan shavings, to garnish

1 Cook the pasta in a saucepan of boiling salted water for 8–10 minutes, or until "al dente." Drain well.

2 Meanwhile, heat the oil in a large saucepan and sauté the garlic and onion for 1 minute.

3 Add the sliced mushrooms and cook for 2 minutes, stirring occasionally.

4 Add the spinach and cook for 4–5 minutes, or until the spinach has wilted.

5 Stir in the pine nuts and wine, season well with salt and pepper, and cook for 1 minute.

6 Transfer the pasta to a warm serving bowl and toss the sauce into it, mixing well. Garnish with shavings of Parmesan cheese and serve at once.

COOK'S TIP

*"Al dente" means that the pasta
should be tender but still
have a bite to it.*

COOK'S TIP

*Freshly grate a little
nutmeg over the dish for
extra flavor, as it is
particularly good with spinach.*

Bean Curd & Vegetable Stir-Fry

*This is a quick dish to prepare, making it ideal as a midweek supper dish,
after a busy day at work!*

Serves 4

INGREDIENTS

1¼ cups diced potatoes
1 tablespoon olive oil
1 red onion, sliced
8 ounces firm bean curd, diced
2 zucchini, diced
8 canned artichoke hearts, halved

²/₃ cup sieved tomatoes
1 teaspoon sugar
2 tablespoons chopped basil
salt and pepper

1 Cook the potatoes in a saucepan of boiling water for 10 minutes. Drain thoroughly and set aside until required.

2 Heat the oil in a large skillet and sauté the red onion for 2 minutes, until the onion has softened, stirring.

3 Stir in the bean curd and zucchini and cook for 3–4 minutes, until they begin to brown slightly. Add the potatoes, stirring to mix.

4 Stir in the artichoke hearts, sieved tomatoes, sugar, and basil, season with salt and pepper, and cook for a further 5 minutes, stirring well. Transfer the stir-fry to serving dishes and serve at once.

VARIATION

Eggplants could be used instead of the zucchini, if desired.

COOK'S TIP

Canned artichoke hearts should be drained thoroughly and rinsed before use because they often have salt added.

Cantonese Garden Vegetable Stir-Fry

This dish tastes as fresh as it looks. Try to get hold of baby vegetables, as they look and taste so much better in this dish.

Serves 4

INGREDIENTS

2 tablespoons peanut oil
1 teaspoon Chinese five-
   spice powder
2³/₄ ounces baby carrots, halved
2 celery stalks, sliced
2 baby leeks, sliced

1³/₄ ounces snow peas
4 baby zucchini, halved
   lengthwise
8 baby corn
8 ounces firm marinated
   bean curd, diced

4 tablespoons fresh orange juice
1 tablespoon honey
celery leaves and orange zest,
   to garnish
cooked rice or noodles, to serve

1 Heat the oil in a preheated wok until almost smoking. Add the Chinese five-spice powder, carrots, celery, leeks, snow peas, zucchini, and corn and stir-fry for 3–4 minutes over medium heat.

2 Add the bean curd and cook for a further 2 minutes, stirring constantly.

3 Stir in the orange juice and honey, reduce the heat, and cook for 1–2 minutes.

4 Transfer the stir-fry to a serving dish, garnish with celery leaves and orange zest, and serve with rice or noodles.

COOK'S TIP

Chinese five-spice powder is a mixture of fennel, star anise, cinnamon bark, cloves, and Szechuan pepper. It is very pungent, so should be used sparingly. If kept in an airtight container, it will keep indefinitely.

VARIATION

Lemon juice would be just as delicious as the orange juice in this recipe, but use 3 tablespoons instead of 4 tablespoons.

Risotto Verde

Risotto is an Italian dish which is easy to make and uses a round-grain rice, onion, and garlic as a base for a range of savory recipes.

Serves 4

INGREDIENTS

$7\frac{1}{2}$ cups vegetable stock
2 tablespoons olive oil
2 garlic cloves, crushed
2 leeks, shredded
$1\frac{1}{4}$ cups risotto (arborio) rice
$1\frac{1}{4}$ cups dry white wine

4 tablespoons chopped mixed herbs
8 ounces baby spinach
3 tablespoons plain yogurt
salt and pepper
shredded leek, to garnish

1 Pour the stock into a large saucepan and bring to a boil. Reduce the heat to a simmer.

2 Meanwhile, heat the oil in a separate pan and sauté the garlic and leeks for 2–3 minutes, until softened.

3 Stir in the rice and cook for 2 minutes, stirring, until well coated.

4 Pour in half of the wine and a little of the hot stock. Cook over a gentle heat until all of the liquid has been absorbed. Add the remaining stock and wine and cook over low heat for 25 minutes, or until the rice is creamy.

5 Stir in the chopped mixed herbs and baby spinach, season well with salt and pepper, and cook for 2 minutes.

6 Stir in the plain yogurt, transfer to a warm serving dish, garnish with the shredded leek and serve at once.

COOK'S TIP

Do not hurry the process of cooking the risotto, as the rice must absorb the liquid slowly in order for it to reach the correct consistency.

Baked Pasta in Tomato Sauce

This pasta dish is baked in a heatproof bowl and cut into slices for serving.
It looks and tastes terrific, and is perfect when you want to impress.

Serves 8

INGREDIENTS

1 cup pasta shapes,
  such as penne or casareccia
1 tablespoon olive oil
1 leek, chopped
3 garlic cloves, crushed
1 green bell pepper, chopped
14 ounce can chopped tomatoes

2 tablespoons chopped, pitted
  black olives
2 eggs, beaten
1 tablespoon chopped basil

TOMATO SAUCE:
1 tablespoon olive oil

1 onion, chopped
8 ounce can chopped tomatoes
1 teaspoon sugar
2 tablespoons tomato paste
$2/3$ cup vegetable stock
salt and pepper

1 Cook the pasta in a saucepan of boiling salted water for 8 minutes. Drain thoroughly.

2 Meanwhile, heat the oil in a saucepan and sauté the leek and garlic for 2 minutes, stirring. Add the bell pepper, tomatoes, and olives and cook for a further 5 minutes.

3 Remove the pan from the heat and stir in the pasta, beaten eggs, and basil. Season well, and spoon into a lightly greased 4-cup ovenproof bowl.

4 Place the bowl in a roasting pan and half fill the pan with boiling water. Cover and cook in a preheated oven at 350°F for 40 minutes, until set.

5 To make the sauce, heat the oil in a pan and sauté the onion for 2 minutes. Add the remaining ingredients and cook for 10 minutes. Put the sauce in a food processor or blender and process until smooth. Return to a clean saucepan and heat until hot.

6 Turn the pasta out of the bowl onto a warm serving plate. Slice and serve at once with the tomato sauce.

Spaghetti with Pear & Walnut Sauce

This is quite an unusual combination of ingredients in a savory dish,
but is absolutely wonderful tossed into a fine pasta, such as spaghetti.

Serves 4

INGREDIENTS

8 ounces spaghetti
2 small ripe pears, peeled and sliced
$2/3$ cup vegetable stock
6 tablespoons dry white wine
2 tablespoons butter
1 tablespoon olive oil

1 red onion, quartered and sliced
1 garlic clove, crushed
$1/2$ cup walnut halves
2 tablespoons chopped oregano
1 tablespoon lemon juice
$3/4$ cup blue cheese

salt and pepper
fresh oregano sprigs, to garnish

1 Cook the pasta in a saucepan of boiling salted water for 8–10 minutes, or until "al dente." Drain thoroughly and keep warm until required.

2 Meanwhile, place the pears in a pan and pour over the stock and wine. Poach the pears over gentle heat for 10 minutes. Drain and reserve the cooking liquid and pears.

3 Heat the butter and oil in a saucepan until the butter melts, then sauté the onion and garlic for 2–3 minutes, stirring.

4 Add the walnuts, oregano, and lemon juice, stirring.

5 Stir in the reserved pears with 4 tablespoons of the poaching liquid.

6 Crumble the dolcelatte cheese into the pan and cook over gentle heat, stirring occasionally, for 1–2 minutes, or until the cheese just begins to melt. Season the sauce with salt and pepper to taste.

7 Toss the pasta into the sauce, garnish, and serve.

COOK'S TIP

You can use any good-flavored blue cheese for this dish. Varieties to try are Roquefort, which has a very strong flavor, gorgonzola, or Stilton.

Side Dishes

If you are running short of ideas for interesting side dishes to serve with your main meals, these recipes will be a welcome inspiration. An ideal accompaniment complements the main dish both visually and nutritionally. Many main dishes will be rich in protein, therefore the side dishes in this chapter have been created to be a little lighter in texture, but still packed full of color and flavor. They have been cooked in many different ways—there are bakes, fries, steamed vegetables, and braises, all of which are perfect accompaniments for all occasions.

This chapter also contains a selection of delicious salads, which are bursting with flavor and color. Make one of these salads to accompany your main meal, or make larger portions to serve alone. Choose the right salad to serve with your main meal—make sure that the flavors and textures complement rather than clash with one another. The secret of a successful salad relies on one important aspect: the freshness of the ingredients. Try some of of the ideas in this chapter and discover some sensational side dishes to add to your repertoire.

Cheese & Potato Layer Bake

*This really is a great side dish, perfect for serving
with main meals cooked in the oven.*

Serves 4

INGREDIENTS

1 pound potatoes
1 leek, sliced
3 garlic cloves, crushed
$\frac{1}{2}$ cup grated vegetarian
  cheddar, cheese
$\frac{1}{2}$ cup grated mozzarella cheese

$\frac{1}{4}$ cup grated Parmesan cheese
2 tablespoons chopped parsley
$\frac{2}{3}$ cup light cream
$\frac{2}{3}$ cup milk

salt and pepper
freshly chopped flat leaf parsley,
  to garnish

1 Cook the potatoes in a saucepan of boiling salted water for 10 minutes. Drain well.

2 Cut the potatoes into thin slices. Arrange a layer of potatoes in the base of an ovenproof dish. Layer with a little of the leek, garlic, cheeses, and parsley. Season well.

3 Repeat the layers until all of the ingredients have been used, finishing with a layer of cheese on top.

4 Mix the cream and milk together, season with salt and pepper to taste, and pour the mixture over the potato layers.

5 Cook in a preheated oven at 325°F for about 1–1¼ hours, or until the cheese is golden brown and bubbling and the potatoes are cooked through and tender.

6 Garnish with freshly chopped flat leaf parsley and serve at once straight from the dish.

COOK'S TIP

There is an Italian Parmesan called Grano Padano which is usually vegetarian. As Parmesan quickly loses its "bite", it is best to buy it in small quantities and grate only as much as you need. Wrap the rest in foil and store in the refrigerator.

Cauliflower & Broccoli with Herb Sauce

Whole baby cauliflowers are used in this recipe. Try to find them if you can; if not, use large bunches of florets.

Serves 4

INGREDIENTS

2 baby cauliflowers
8 ounces broccoli
salt and pepper

SAUCE:
8 tablespoons olive oil
4 tablespoons butter or
   vegetarian margarine

2 teaspoons grated ginger root
juice and rind of 2 lemons
5 tablespoons chopped cilantro
5 tablespoons grated cheddar

1 Using a sharp knife, cut the cauliflowers in half and the broccoli into very large florets.

2 Cook the cauliflower and broccoli in a saucepan of boiling salted water for about 10 minutes. Drain well, transfer to a shallow ovenproof dish, and keep warm until required.

3 To make the sauce, put the oil and butter or vegetarian margarine in a pan and heat gently until the butter melts. Add the grated ginger root, lemon juice, lemon rind, and chopped cilantro and simmer for 2–3 minutes, stirring occasionally.

4 Season the sauce with salt and pepper to taste, then pour it over the vegetables in the dish and sprinkle the cheese on top.

5 Cook under a preheated broiler for 2–3 minutes, or until the cheese is bubbling and golden. Let cool for 1–2 minutes and then serve.

VARIATION

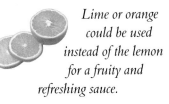

Lime or orange could be used instead of the lemon for a fruity and refreshing sauce.

Indian Spiced Potatoes & Spinach

*This is a classic Indian accompaniment for
curries or plainer main vegetable dishes.*

Serves 4

INGREDIENTS

3 tablespoons vegetable oil	1 teaspoon ground cumin	salt and pepper
1 red onion, sliced	$^2/_3$ cup vegetable stock	
2 garlic cloves, crushed	$^2/_3$ cup diced potatoes	
$^1/_2$ teaspoon chili powder	1 pound baby spinach	
2 teaspoons ground coriander	1 red chili, sliced	

1 Heat the oil in a large, heavy-based skillet and sauté the onion and garlic, stirring occasionally, for 2–3 minutes, until soft and translucent.

2 Stir in the chili powder, ground coriander, and cumin and cook for a further 30 seconds.

3 Add the vegetable stock, potato, and spinach and bring to a boil. Reduce the heat, cover the skillet, and simmer for about 10 minutes, or until the potatoes are cooked through.

4 Uncover, season to taste, add the chili, and cook for a further 2–3 minutes. Serve.

COOK'S TIP

Be very careful when handling chilies—never touch your face or eyes, as the juices can be very painful, and always wash your hands thoroughly after preparing chiles. The seeds are the hottest part of the chili, but have less flavor, so these are usually removed before use.

VARIATION

Add other vegetables, such as chopped tomatoes, for color and flavor.

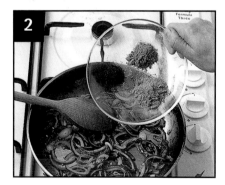

Spicy Peas & Spinach

This is quite a filling dish, and should be served with a light main course.
Green split peas are a type of legume.

Serves 4

INGREDIENTS

1¼ cups green split peas
2 pounds spinach
4 tablespoons vegetable oil
1 onion, halved and sliced
1 teaspoon grated ginger root
1 teaspoon ground cumin

½ teaspoon chili powder
½ teaspoon ground coriander
2 garlic cloves, crushed
1¼ cups vegetable stock

salt and pepper
fresh cilantro sprigs and lime wedges,
  to garnish

1 Rinse the peas under cold running water. Transfer to a mixing bowl, cover with cold water, and set aside to soak for 2 hours. Drain well.

2 Meanwhile, cook the spinach in a large saucepan for 5 minutes, until wilted. Drain well and roughly chop.

3 Heat the oil in a large saucepan and add the onion, spices, and garlic. Sauté for 2–3 minutes, stirring well.

4 Add the peas and spinach and stir in the stock. Cover and simmer for 10–15 minutes, or until the peas are cooked and the liquid has been absorbed. Season with salt and pepper to taste, garnish, and serve.

VARIATION

If you do not have time to soak the green peas, canned lentils are a good substitute, but remember to drain and rinse them first.

COOK'S TIP

Once the peas have been added, stir occasionally to prevent them from sticking to the pan.

Beans in Lemon & Herb Sauce

*Use a variety of beans if possible, although this recipe is
perfectly acceptable with just one type of bean.*

Serves 4

INGREDIENTS

2 pounds mixed green beans,
  such as fava beans,
  green beans, string beans
$1/2$ cup butter or
  vegetarian margarine
4 teaspoons all-purpose flour

$1^{1}/_{4}$ cups vegetable stock
6 tablespoons dry white wine
6 tablespoons light cream
3 tablespoons chopped mixed herbs
2 tablespoons lemon juice
rind of 1 lemon

salt and pepper

1 Cook the beans in a saucepan of boiling salted water for 10 minutes, or until tender. Drain and place in a warm serving dish.

2 Meanwhile, melt the butter in a saucepan. Add the flour and cook for 1 minute. Remove the pan from the heat and gradually stir in the stock and wine. Return the pan to the heat and bring to a boil.

3 Remove the pan from the heat once again and stir in the light cream, mixed herbs, lemon juice, and zest. Season with salt and pepper to taste. Pour the sauce over the beans, mixing well. Serve at once.

VARIATION

Use lime rind and juice instead of lemon for an alternative citrus flavor. Replace the light cream with plain yogurt for a healthier version of this dish.

COOK'S TIP

Use a wide variety of herbs for flavor, such as rosemary, thyme, tarragon, and sage.

Curried Cauliflower & Spinach

The contrast in color in this recipe makes it very appealing to the eye, especially as the cauliflower is lightly colored with yellow turmeric.

Serves 4

INGREDIENTS

1 medium cauliflower	2 garlic cloves, crushed	salt and pepper
6 tablespoons vegetable oil	1 onion, halved and sliced	cilantro sprigs, to garnish
1 teaspoon mustard seeds	1 green chili, sliced	
1 teaspoon ground cumin	1 pound spinach	
1 teaspoon garam masala	6 tablespoons vegetable stock	
1 teaspoon turmeric	1 tablespoon chopped cilantro	

1 Break the cauliflower into small florets.

2 Heat the oil in a deep flameproof casserole. Add the mustard seeds and cook until they begin to pop.

3 Stir in the remaining spices, the garlic, onion, and chili and cook for 2–3 minutes, stirring.

4 Add the cauliflower, spinach, vegetable stock, cilantro, and seasoning and cook over gentle heat for 15 minutes, or until the cauliflower is tender. Uncover the dish and boil for 1 minute to thicken the juices. Garnish and serve at once.

COOK'S TIP

Mustard seeds are used throughout India and are particularly popular in southern vegetarian cooking. They are fried in oil first to bring out their flavor before the other ingredients are added.

VARIATION

Broccoli may be used instead of the cauliflower, if desired.

Eggplant & Zucchini Galette

This is a dish of eggplant and zucchini layered with a quick tomato sauce and melted cheese.

Serves 4

INGREDIENTS

2 large eggplants, sliced
4 zucchini
2 x 14 ounce cans chopped
   tomatoes, drained
2 tablespoons tomato paste

2 garlic cloves, crushed
4 tablespoons olive oil
1 teaspoon sugar
2 tablespoons chopped basil
olive oil, for frying

8 ounces Mozzarella cheese, sliced
salt and pepper
fresh basil leaves, to garnish

1 Put the eggplant slices in a colander and sprinkle with salt. Set aside to stand for about 30 minutes, then rinse well under cold water, and drain. Thinly slice the zucchini.

2 Meanwhile, put the tomatoes, tomato paste, garlic, olive oil, sugar, and chopped basil into a pan and simmer over low heat for about 20 minutes, or until reduced by half. Season well.

3 Heat 2 tablespoons of olive oil in a large, heavy-based skillet and cook the eggplant slices for about 2–3 minutes, until just beginning to brown. Remove from the skillet.

4 Add a further 2 tablespoons of oil to the skillet and fry the zucchini slices until browned.

5 Place half of the eggplant slices in the base of an ovenproof dish. Top with half of the tomato sauce and the zucchini and then half of the mozzarella.

6 Repeat the layers and bake in a preheated oven at 350°F for 45–50 minutes, or until the vegetables are tender. Garnish with basil leaves and serve.

Baked Celery with Cream & Pecans

This dish is topped with bread crumbs for a crunchy topping, underneath which is hidden a creamy celery and pecan mixture.

Serves 4

INGREDIENTS

1 head of celery
$^1/_2$ teaspoon ground cumin
$^1/_2$ teaspoon ground coriander
1 garlic clove, crushed
1 red onion, thinly sliced
$^1/_2$ cup pecan nut halves

$^2/_3$ cup vegetable stock
$^2/_3$ cup light cream
1 cup fresh whole wheat
   bread crumbs

$^1/_4$ cup freshly grated
   Parmesan cheese
salt and pepper
celery leaves, to garnish

1 Trim the celery and cut into matchsticks. Place the celery in an ovenproof dish with the ground cumin, coriander, garlic, onion, and pecan nuts.

2 Mix the stock and cream together and pour it over the vegetables. Season with salt and pepper to taste.

3 Mix the bread crumbs and grated cheese together and sprinkle over the top to cover the vegetables completely.

4 Cook in a preheated oven at 400°F for 40 minutes, or until the vegetables are tender and the top crispy. Garnish with celery leaves and serve at once.

VARIATION

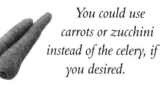

You could use carrots or zucchini instead of the celery, if you desired.

COOK'S TIP

Once grated, Parmesan cheese quickly loses its "bite" so it is best to grate only the amount you need for the recipe. Wrap the rest tightly in foil and it will keep for several months in the refrigerator.

Pepperonata

A delicious mixture of bell peppers and onions, cooked with tomatoes and herbs for a rich side dish.

Serves 4

INGREDIENTS

4 tablespoons olive oil
1 onion, halved and finely sliced
2 red bell peppers, cut into strips
2 green bell peppers, cut into strips
2 yellow bell peppers, cut into strips
2 garlic cloves, crushed

2 x 14 ounce cans chopped
    tomatoes, drained
2 tablespoons chopped cilantro
2 tablespoons chopped pitted
    black olives
salt and pepper

1 Heat the oil in a large skillet. Add the onion and sauté for 5 minutes, stirring, until just beginning to color.

2 Add the bell peppers and garlic to the skillet and cook for a further 3–4 minutes.

3 Stir in the tomatoes and cilantro and season with salt and pepper. Cover the skillet and cook the vegetables gently for about 30 minutes, or until the mixture is dry.

4 Stir in the pitted black olives and serve the pepperonata at once.

COOK'S TIP

Stir the vegetables occasionally during the 30 minutes cooking time to prevent them from sticking to the bottom of the skillet. If the liquid has not evaporated by the end of the cooking time, remove the lid and boil rapidly until the dish is dry.

VARIATION

If you don't like the distinctive flavor of fresh cilantro, you can replace it with 2 tablespoons chopped fresh flat leaf parsley. Use green olives instead of black ones, if desired.

Soufflèd Cheese Potatoes

*These small potato chunks are mixed in a creamy cheese sauce and
fried in oil until deliciously golden brown.*

Serves 4

INGREDIENTS

2 pounds potatoes, cut into chunks
$^{2}/_{3}$ cup heavy cream
$^{3}/_{4}$ cup grated Swiss cheese
pinch of cayenne pepper
2 egg whites
oil, for deep-frying

salt and pepper
chopped flat leaf parsley and grated
    vegetarian cheese, to garnish

1 Cook the potatoes in a saucepan of boiling salted water for 10 minutes. Drain well and pat dry with absorbent paper towels. Set aside until required.

2 Mix together the heavy cream and Swiss cheese in a large bowl. Stir in the cayenne pepper and season with salt and pepper to taste.

3 Whisk the egg whites until stiff peaks form. Fold into the cheese mixture until fully incorporated.

4 Add the cooked potatoes, turning to coat thoroughly in the mixture.

5 Heat the oil for deep-frying to 350°F or until a cube of bread browns in 30 seconds. Remove the potatoes from the cheese mixture with a slotted spoon and cook in the oil, in batches, for 3–4 minutes, or until golden brown.

6 Transfer the potatoes to a serving dish and garnish with parsley and grated cheese. Serve.

VARIATION

*Add other flavorings,
such as grated nutmeg
or curry powder, to the
cream and cheese.*

Bulgur Pilau

Bulgur wheat is very easy to use and is a delicious alternative to rice, having a distinctive nutty flavor.

Serves 4

INGREDIENTS

6 tablespoons butter or
   vegetarian margarine
1 red onion, halved and sliced
2 garlic cloves, crushed
2 cups bulgur wheat
6 ounces tomatoes, seeded
   and chopped

1³/4 ounces baby corn,
   halved lengthwise
2³/4 ounces small broccoli florets
3³/4 cups vegetable stock
2 tablespoons honey
¹/3 cup golden raisins
¹/2 cup pine nuts

¹/2 teaspoon ground cinnamon
¹/2 teaspoon ground cumin
salt and pepper
sliced scallions,
   to garnish

1 Melt the butter or vegetarian margarine in a large flameproof casserole.

2 Add the onion and garlic and sauté for 2–3 minutes, stirring occasionally.

3 Add the bulgur wheat, tomatoes, corn, broccoli florets, and stock and bring to a boil. Reduce the heat, cover, and simmer for 15–20 minutes, stirring occasionally.

4 Stir in the honey, golden raisins, pine nuts, ground cinnamon, cumin, and salt and pepper to taste, mixing well. Remove the casserole from the heat, cover, and set aside for 10 minutes.

5 Spoon the bulgur pilau into a warm serving dish.

6 Garnish the bulgur pilau with sliced scallions and serve at once.

COOK'S TIP

The dish is left to stand for 10 minutes in order for the bulgur to finish cooking and the flavors to mingle.

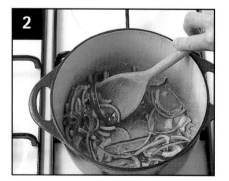

Pesto Potatoes

Pesto sauce is more commonly used as a pasta sauce, but is delicious served over potatoes as well.

Serves 4

INGREDIENTS

2 pounds small new potatoes
$^1/_2$ cup fresh basil
2 tablespoons pine nuts
3 garlic cloves, crushed
$^1/_2$ cup olive oil

$^3/_4$ cup freshly grated
Parmesan cheese and Pecorino
cheese, mixed

salt and pepper
fresh basil sprigs, to garnish

1 Cook the potatoes in a saucepan of boiling salted water for 15 minutes, or until tender. Drain well, transfer to a warm serving dish, and keep warm until required.

2 Meanwhile, put the basil, pine nuts, garlic, and a little salt and pepper to taste in a food processor. Process for 30 seconds, adding the oil gradually, until smooth.

3 Remove the mixture from the food processor and place in a mixing bowl. Stir in the grated Parmesan and Pecorino cheeses.

4 Spoon the pesto sauce over the potatoes and mix well. Garnish with fresh basil sprigs and serve at once.

COOK'S TIP

Store this pesto sauce in an airtight container for up to a week in the refrigerator. It can also be frozen (before adding the cheeses) for several months.

COOK'S TIP

This sauce would also make a great dressing for crisp salad greens.

Carrot, Orange, & Poppy Seed Bake

The poppy seeds add texture and flavor to this recipe,
and counteract the slightly sweet flavor of the carrots.

Serves 4

INGREDIENTS

$1^1/_2$ pounds carrots, cut
   into thin strips
1 leek, sliced
$1^1/_4$ cups fresh
   orange juice
2 tablespoons honey

1 garlic clove, crushed
1 teaspoon pumpkin pie spice
2 teaspoons chopped thyme
1 tablespoon poppy seeds

salt and pepper
fresh thyme sprigs and orange
   rind, to garnish

1 Cook the carrots and leek in a large saucepan of boiling lightly salted water for 5–6 minutes. Drain well and transfer to a shallow ovenproof dish until required.

2 Mix together the orange juice, honey, garlic, pumpkin pie spice, and thyme and pour the mixture over the vegetables. Add salt and pepper to taste.

3 Cover the ovenproof dish and cook in a preheated oven at 350°F for 30 minutes, or until the vegetables are tender.

4 Remove the lid and sprinkle with poppy seeds. Garnish with fresh thyme sprigs and orange rind and serve.

VARIATION

If desired, use 2 teaspoons cumin instead of the pumpkin pie spice and omit the thyme, as cumin works particularly well with carrots.

COOK'S TIP

Lemon or lime juice could be used instead of the orange juice if desired. Garnish with lemon or lime rind.

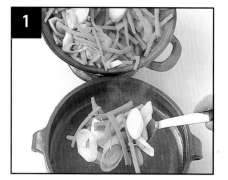

Greek Green Beans

This dish contains many Greek flavors, such as lemon, garlic, oregano, and olives, for a really tasty recipe.

Serves 4

INGREDIENTS

14 ounce can navy beans, drained
1 tablespoon olive oil
3 garlic cloves, crushed
2 cups vegetable stock
1 bay leaf
2 sprigs oregano

1 tablespoon tomato paste
juice of 1 lemon
1 small red onion, chopped
$^1/_4$ cup pitted black olives, halved
salt and pepper

1 Put the navy beans in a large flameproof casserole.

2 Add the olive oil and crushed garlic and cook over gentle heat, stirring occasionally, for 4–5 minutes, until soft and translucent.

3 Add the vegetable stock, bay leaf, oregano, tomato paste, lemon juice and red onion, cover, and simmer, stirring occasionally for about 1 hour, or until the sauce has thickened.

4 Stir in the olives, season with salt and pepper to taste, and serve.

VARIATION

You can substitute other canned beans for the navy beans—try cannellini or black-eyed peas, or garbanzo beans instead. Remember to drain and rinse them thoroughly before use, as canned beans often have sugar or salt added.

COOK'S TIP

This dish may be made in advance and served cold with crusty bread, if desired.

Sweet & Sour Eggplant

*This is a dish of Persian origin, not Chinese as it sounds. Eggplant are fried
and mixed with tomatoes, mint, sugar, and vinegar for a really intense flavor.*

Serves 4

INGREDIENTS

2 large eggplants
6 tablespoons olive oil
4 garlic cloves, crushed
1 onion, cut into eight
4 large tomatoes,
   seeded and chopped

3 tablespoons chopped mint
$^2/_3$ cup vegetable stock
4 teaspoons brown sugar
2 tablespoons red
   wine vinegar
1 teaspoon chili flakes

salt and pepper
fresh mint sprigs, to garnish

1 Using a sharp knife, cut the eggplants into cubes. Put them in a colander, sprinkle with salt, and let stand for 30 minutes. Rinse thoroughly under cold running water and drain well. This process removes all the bitter juices from the eggplants. Pat thoroughly dry with absorbent paper towels.

2 Heat the oil in a large skillet and sauté the eggplant cubes, stirring constantly, for about 1–2 minutes.

3 Stir in the garlic and onion and cook for a further 2–3 minutes.

4 Stir in the tomatoes, mint, and stock, cover, and cook for 15–20 minutes, or until the vegetables are tender.

5 Stir in the brown sugar, red wine vinegar, and chili flakes, season with salt and pepper to taste, and cook for 2–3 minutes. Garnish the eggplant with fresh mint sprigs and serve.

COOK'S TIP

Mint is a popular herb in Middle Eastern cooking. It is a useful herb to grow yourself, as it can be added to a variety of dishes, particularly salads and vegetable dishes. It can be grown easily in a garden or window box.

Mini Vegetable Puff Pastries

*These are ideal with a more formal meal as they take
a little time to prepare and look really impressive.*

Serves 4

INGREDIENTS

1 pound puff pastry
1 egg, beaten

FILLING:
8 ounces sweet potato, cubed

3¹/₂ ounces baby asparagus spears
2 tablespoons butter or vegetarian
   margarine
1 leek, sliced
2 small mushrooms, sliced

1 teaspoon lime juice
1 teaspoon chopped thyme
pinch of dried mustard
salt and pepper

1 Cut the pastry into 4 equal pieces. Roll each piece out on a lightly floured counter to form a 5-inch square. Place on dampened cookie sheets and score a smaller 2¹/₂-inch square inside with the point of a sharp knife.

2 Brush with beaten egg to glaze and cook in a preheated oven at 400°F for 20 minutes, or until the pastry has risen and is golden brown.

3 Remove the pastry squares from the oven, then carefully cut out the central square of pastry, lift it out, and reserve.

4 To make the filling, cook the sweet potato in a saucepan of boiling water for 15 minutes, then drain well. Blanch the asparagus in a saucepan of boiling water for 10 minutes, or until tender. Drain and reserve.

5 Melt the butter or margarine in a saucepan and sauté the leek and mushrooms for 2–3 minutes. Add the lime juice, thyme, and mustard, season well, and stir in the sweet potatoes and asparagus. Spoon into the pastry cases, top with the reserved pastry squares, and serve at once.

COOK'S TIP

*Use a colorful selection
of any vegetables you have at hand
for this recipe.*

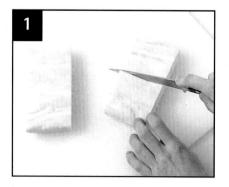

Eggplant Salad

*This salad uses sesame seed paste as a flavoring
for the dressing, which complements the eggplant.*

Serves 4

INGREDIENTS

1 large eggplant
3 tablespoons sesame seed paste
juice and rind of 1 lemon
1 garlic clove, crushed
pinch of paprika
1 tablespoon chopped cilantro

salt and pepper
lettuce leaves

GARNISH:
strips of pimiento
lemon wedges
toasted sesame seeds

1 Cut the eggplant in half, place in a colander, and sprinkle with salt. Set aside for 30 minutes to allow the bitter juices to drain. Rinse thoroughly under cold running water and drain well. Pat thoroughly dry with paper towels.

2 Place the eggplant halves, skin side uppermost, on an oiled cookie sheet. Bake in a preheated oven at 450°F for 10–15 minutes. Remove from the oven and set aside to cool.

3 Cut the eggplant into cubes and set aside until required. Mix the sesame seed paste, lemon juice and rind, garlic, paprika, and cilantro together. Season to taste with salt and pepper and stir in the eggplant.

4 Line a serving dish with lettuce leaves and spoon the eggplant mixture into the center. Garnish the salad with slices of pimiento, lemon wedges, and toasted sesame seeds and serve at once.

COOK'S TIP

Sesame seed paste, also called tahini, is a nutty-flavored sauce available from most health food shops. It is good served with many Middle Eastern dishes.

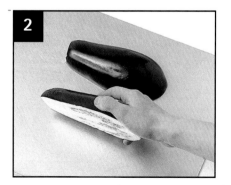

Salad with Garlic & Yogurt Dressing

This is a very quick and refreshing salad using a whole range of colorful ingredients which make it look as good as it tastes.

Serves 4

INGREDIENTS

$2^3/_4$ ounces cucumber,
   cut into batons
6 scallions, halved
2 tomatoes, seeded
   and cut into eight
1 yellow bell pepper, cut into strips
2 celery stalks, cut into strips

4 radishes, quartered
$2^3/_4$ ounces arugula
1 tablespoon chopped mint, to serve

DRESSING:
2 tablespoons lemon juice
1 garlic clove, crushed
$^2/_3$ cup plain yogurt
2 tablespoons olive oil
salt and pepper

1 Mix the cucumber, scallions, tomatoes, bell pepper, celery, radishes, and arugula together in a large serving bowl.

2 To make the dressing, stir the lemon juice, garlic, plain yogurt, and olive oil together. Season well with salt and pepper to taste.

3 Spoon the dressing over the salad and toss well to coat thoroughly.

4 Sprinkle the salad with chopped mint and serve.

COOK'S TIP

Arugula has a distinct warm, peppery flavor which is ideal in salads. Once you have grown it in your garden or greenhouse, you will always have plenty as it re-seeds all over the place! If arugula is unavailable, spinach makes a good substitute.

COOK'S TIP

Do not toss the dressing into the salad until just before serving, otherwise it will turn soggy.

Zucchini, Yogurt, & Mint Salad

This salad uses lots of green-colored ingredients which look and taste wonderful with the minty yogurt dressing.

Serves 4

INGREDIENTS

2 zucchini, cut into sticks
3^1/$_2$ ounces green beans,
   cut into three
1 green bell pepper, cut into strips
2 celery stalks, sliced
1 bunch watercress

DRESSING:
^{3}/$_4$ cup plain yogurt
1 garlic clove, crushed
2 tablespoons chopped mint
pepper

1 Cook the zucchini and green beans in a saucepan of salted boiling water for 7–8 minutes. Drain well and set aside to cool completely.

2 Mix the zucchini and green beans with the bell pepper, celery, and watercress in a large serving bowl.

3 To make the dressing, mix together the plain yogurt, garlic, and chopped mint in a bowl until thoroughly combined.

Season with pepper to taste.

4 Spoon the dressing onto the salad and serve at once.

COOK'S TIP

The salad must be served as soon as the yogurt dressing has been added—the dressing will start to separate if kept for any length of time.

COOK'S TIP

Watercress is available all year around. Its fresh peppery flavor makes it a delicious addition to many salads.

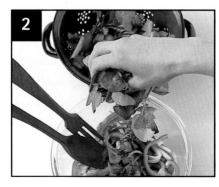

Bean, Avocado, & Tomato Salad

This is a colorful salad with a Mexican theme, using beans, tomatoes, and avocado.
The chili dressing adds a little kick.

Serves 4

INGREDIENTS

red butter lettuce	DRESSING:	1 tablespoon chopped parsley
2 ripe avocados	4 tablespoons olive oil	
2 teaspoons lemon juice	dash of chili oil	
4 medium tomatoes	2 tablespoons garlic wine vinegar	
1 onion	pinch of sugar	
2 cups mixed canned beans, drained	pinch of chili powder	

1 Line a serving bowl with the lettuce.

2 Using a sharp knife, thinly slice the avocados and sprinkle with the lemon juice.

3 Thinly slice the tomatoes and onion. Arrange the avocado, tomatoes, and onion around the salad bowl, leaving a space in the center.

4 Spoon the beans into the center of the salad and whisk the dressing ingredients together. Pour the dressing over the salad and serve.

COOK'S TIP

The lemon juice is sprinkled onto the avocados to prevent discoloration when in contact with the air. For this reason the salad should be prepared, assembled, and served quite quickly.

COOK'S TIP

Instead of whisking the dressing, place all the ingredients in a screw-top jar and shake vigorously. Any leftover dressing can then be kept and stored in the same jar.

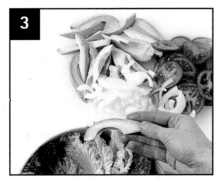

Gado Gado

This is a very well known Indonesian salad of mixed vegetables with a peanut dressing.

Serves 4

INGREDIENTS

1 cup white cabbage, shredded
$3^1/_2$ ounces green beans,
   cut into 3
$3^1/_2$ ounces carrots,
   cut into matchsticks
$3^1/_2$ ounces cauliflower florets
$3^1/_2$ ounces bean sprouts

DRESSING:
$^1/_2$ cup vegetable oil
1 cup unsalted peanuts
2 garlic cloves, crushed
1 small onion, finely chopped
$^1/_2$ teaspoon chili powder
$^1/_3$ teaspoon light brown sugar

2 cups water
juice of $^1/_2$ lemon
salt
sliced scallions, to garnish

1 Cook the vegetables separately in saucepans of salted boiling water for 4–5 minutes, drain well, and chill in the refrigerator.

2 To make the dressing, heat the oil in a skillet and fry the peanuts for 3–4 minutes, turning.

3 Remove from the skillet with a slotted spoon and drain on absorbent paper towels. Grind the peanuts in a blender or crush with the end of a rolling pin until a fine mixture is formed.

4 Pour all but 1 tablespoon of the oil from the skillet and fry the garlic and onion for 1 minute. Add the chili powder, sugar, a pinch of salt, and the water and bring to a boil.

5 Stir in the peanuts. Reduce the heat and simmer for 4–5 minutes, until thickened. Add the lemon juice and let cool.

6 Arrange the vegetables in a serving dish and spoon the peanut dressing into the center. Garnish and serve.

COOK'S TIP

If necessary, you can prepare the peanut dressing in advance and then store it in the refrigerator for up to 12 hours before serving.

Broiled Vegetable Salad with Mustard Dressing

The vegetables for this dish are best prepared well in advance and chilled before serving.

Serves 4

INGREDIENTS

1 zucchini, sliced
1 yellow bell pepper, sliced
1 eggplant, sliced
1 fennel bulb, cut into eight
1 red onion, cut into eight
16 cherry tomatoes
3 tablespoons olive oil

1 garlic clove, crushed
fresh rosemary sprigs, to garnish

DRESSING:
4 tablespoons olive oil
2 tablespoons balsamic vinegar
2 teaspoons chopped rosemary

1 teaspoon Dijon mustard
1 teaspoon clear honey
2 teaspoons lemon juice

1 Put all of the vegetables, except for the cherry tomatoes, onto a cookie sheet.

2 Mix together the olive oil and garlic and brush the mixture over the vegetables. Cook under a preheated broiler for 10 minutes, until tender and just beginning to char and blister. Set aside to cool. Spoon the vegetables into a serving bowl.

3 Mix the dressing ingredients and pour it over the vegetables. Cover and chill for 1 hour. Garnish and serve.

COOK'S TIP

This dish could also be served warm—heat the dressing in a pan and then toss into the vegetables.

COOK'S TIP

Balsamic vinegar is made in and around Modena in Italy. It is dark and mellow with a sweet-sour flavor. Although it is rather expensive, you need only a small amount to give a wonderful taste to the dressing. If it is unavailable, use sherry vinegar or white wine vinegar instead.

Red Cabbage & Pear Salad

Red cabbage is much underused—it is a colorful and tasty ingredient which is perfect with fruits, such as pears or apples.

Serves 4

INGREDIENTS

4 cups finely shredded
  red cabbage
2 bosc pears, thinly sliced
4 scallions, sliced
1 carrot, grated
fresh chives, to garnish

lettuce leaves, to serve

DRESSING:
4 tablespoons pear juice
1 teaspoon wholegrain mustard
3 tablespoons olive oil

1 tablespoon garlic wine vinegar
1 tablespoon chopped chives

1 Put the cabbage, pears, and scallions in a bowl and mix thoroughly together.

2 Line a serving dish with lettuce leaves and spoon the cabbage and pear mixture into the center.

3 Sprinkle the carrot into the center of the cabbage to form a domed pile.

4 To make the dressing, mix together the pear juice, wholegrain mustard, olive oil, garlic wine vinegar, and chives.

5 Pour the dressing over the salad, toss to mix, garnish, and serve at once.

VARIATION

Experiment with different types of salad greens. The slightly bitter flavor of endive or radicchio would work well with the sweetness of the pears.

COOK'S TIP

Mix the salad just before serving to prevent the color from the red cabbage bleeding into the other ingredients.

Alfalfa, Beet, & Spinach Salad

*This is a really refreshing salad that must be assembled just before serving
to prevent all of the ingredients being tainted pink by the beet.*

Serves 4

INGREDIENTS

3$\frac{1}{2}$ ounces baby spinach
2$\frac{3}{4}$ ounces alfalfa sprouts
2 celery stalks, sliced
4 cooked beets, cut into eight

DRESSING:
4 tablespoons olive oil
6 teaspoons garlic wine vinegar
1 garlic clove, crushed

2 teaspoons honey
1 tablespoon chopped chives

1 Place the spinach and alfalfa sprouts in a large bowl and mix together.

2 Add the celery and mix well.

3 Toss in the beet and mix well.

4 To make the dressing, mix the oil, wine vinegar, garlic, honey, and chopped chives.

5 Pour the dressing over the salad, toss thoroughly, and serve at once.

VARIATION

Add the segments of 1 large orange to the salad to make it even more colorful and refreshing. Replace the garlic wine vinegar with a different flavored oil, such as chili or herb, if desired.

COOK'S TIP

If the spinach leaves are too large, tear them up, rather than cutting them, because cutting bruises the leaves.

COOK'S TIP

Alfalfa sprouts should be available from most supermarkets, if not, use bean sprouts instead.

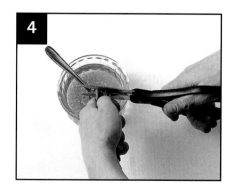

Desserts

Vegetarian or not, confirmed dessert lovers feel a meal is lacking if there isn't a tempting dessert to finish off with. Desserts help to satisfy a deep-seated desire for something sweet, and they make us feel good. However, they are often loaded with fat and sugar, which are notorious for piling on the calories. Some of the recipes in this chapter offer the perfect solution—they are light, but full of flavor, so you can still enjoy that sweet treat without the bulging waistline!

This chapter contains a wonderful selection of irresistible desserts, perfect for rounding off a meal. There are simple fruit fools that are quick to make, cakes, exotic fruit tarts, and all-time favorites, such as chocolate cheesecake and steamed sponge cake. As mentioned in the introduction, vegetarian alternatives may be used for cream and milk in the recipes, and agar (a vegetarian substitute for gelatin) has been used in those recipes that require setting. So take your pick and dip into a delicious dessert!

Raspberry Fool

This dish is very easy to make and can be made in advance and stored in the refrigerator.

Serves 4

INGREDIENTS

1³/4 cups fresh raspberries
1/4 cup confectioners' sugar
1¹/4 cups crème fraîche, plus extra
   to decorate

1/2 teaspoon vanilla extract
2 egg whites
raspberries and lemon balm leaves,
   to decorate

1 Put the raspberries and confectioners' sugar in a food processor or blender and process until smooth.

2 Reserve 1 tablespoon per portion of crème fraîche for decorating.

3 Put the vanilla extract and crème fraîche in a bowl and stir in the raspberry mixture.

4 Whisk the egg whites in a separate mixing bowl until stiff peaks form. Fold the egg whites into the raspberry mixture using a metal spoon, until they are fully incorporated.

5 Spoon the raspberry fool into serving dishes and chill for at least 1 hour. Decorate with the reserved crème fraîche, raspberries, and lemon balm leaves.

COOK'S TIP

Although this dessert is best made with fresh raspberries in season, an acceptable result can be achieved with frozen raspberries, which are available from most supermarkets.

VARIATION

This recipe is also delicious made with strawberries or blackberries.

COOK'S TIP

Crème fraîche is usually vegetarian, however, reduced fat versions tend to contain gelatin, so remember to read the label first.

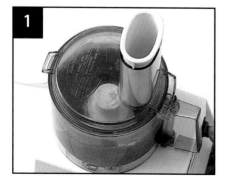

Chocolate Mousse

This is a light and fluffy mousse which is delicious with a fresh fruit sauce. The ingredient agar*, which is used in this recipe, is a seaweed-based vegetarian substitute for gelatin and is widely available.

Serves 8

INGREDIENTS

3^1/$_2$ ounces dark chocolate, melted
1^1/$_4$ cups plain yogurt
^{2}/$_3$ cup cream cheese
4 tablespoons sugar
1 tablespoon orange juice
1 tablespoon brandy

1^1/$_2$ teaspoons agar*
9 tablespoons cold water
2 large egg whites
coarsely grated dark and white
    chocolate and orange zest,
    to decorate

1 Put the chocolate, yogurt, cream cheese, sugar, orange juice, and brandy in a food processor and process for 30 seconds. Transfer to a large bowl.

2 Sprinkle the agar over the water and stir until completely dissolved.

3 In a small pan, bring the agar and water to a boil for 2 minutes. Set aside to cool slightly, then stir into the chocolate mixture.

4 Whisk the egg whites until stiff peaks form, then fold them into the chocolate mixture using a metal spoon.

5 Line a 4-cup loaf pan with plastic wrap. Spoon the mousse into it. Chill for 2 hours in the refrigerator, until set. Turn the mousse out onto a serving plate, decorate with chocolate and orange zest, and serve.

COOK'S TIP

For a quick fruit sauce, process a can of mandarin segments in natural juice in a food processor and press through a strainer. Stir in 1 tablespoon honey and serve with the mousse.

Berry Cheesecake

Use a mixture of berries, such as blueberries, blackberries, raspberries, and strawberries, for a really fruity cheesecake.

Serves 8

INGREDIENTS

BASE:
6 tablespoons vegetarian margarine
6 ounces oatmeal cookies
3/4 cup shredded coconut

TOPPING:
1 1/2 teaspoons agar*
9 tablespoons cold water
1/2 cup evaporated milk
1 egg
6 tablespoons light brown sugar

2 cups soft cream cheese
1 3/4 cups mixed berries
2 tablespoons honey

*See note on page 228.

1 Put the margarine in a saucepan and heat until melted. Put the cookies in a food processor and process until smooth or crush finely with a rolling pin. Stir into the margarine with the coconut.

2 Press the mixture into a base-lined 8-inch springform pan and chill while you are preparing the filling.

3 To make the topping, sprinkle the agar over the water and stir to dissolve. Bring to a boil and boil for 2 minutes. Let cool slightly.

4 Put the milk, egg, sugar, and cream cheese in a bowl and beat until smooth. Stir in 1/4 cup of the berries. Stir in the agar in a stream, stirring constantly, until fully incorporated.

5 Spoon the mixture onto the cookie base, smooth the top, and return to the refrigerator for 2 hours, or until set.

6 Remove the cheesecake from the pan and transfer to a serving plate. Arrange the remaining berries on top of the cheesecake and drizzle the honey over the top. Serve.

COOK'S TIP

Warm the honey slightly to make it runnier and easier to drizzle.

Steamed Coffee Sponge Cake & Sauce

*This sponge pudding is very light and is delicious
with a coffee or chocolate sauce.*

Serves 4

INGREDIENTS

2 tablespoons vegetarian margarine
2 tablespoons soft brown sugar
2 eggs
$^{1}/_{3}$ cup all-purpose flour
$^{3}/_{4}$ teaspoon baking powder

6 tablespoons milk
1 teaspoon coffee extract

SAUCE:
$1^{1}/_{4}$ cups milk
1 tablespoon light brown sugar
1 teaspoon unsweetened cocoa
2 tablespoons cornstarch

1 Lightly grease a 2-cup heatproof bowl. Cream the margarine and sugar until light and fluffy and beat in the eggs.

2 Gradually stir in the flour and baking powder and then the milk and coffee extract to make a smooth batter.

3 Spoon the mixture into the prepared bowl and cover with a pleated piece of baking parchment and then a pleated piece of foil, securing around the bowl with string. Place in a

steamer or large pan and half fill with boiling water. Cover and steam for 1–1$^{1}/_{4}$ hours, or until cooked through.

4 To make the sauce, put the milk, brown sugar, and unsweetened cocoa in a medium saucepan and heat over low heat until the sugar dissolves. Blend the cornstarch with 4 tablespoons of cold water to make a smooth paste and stir into the pan. Bring to a boil, stirring until smooth and thickened. Cook over gentle heat for 1 minute.

5 Turn the pudding out onto a serving plate and spoon the sauce over the top. Serve.

COOK'S TIP

The pudding is covered with pleated paper and foil to allow it to rise. The foil will react with the steam and must therefore not be placed directly against the pudding.

Fruit Brûlée

This is a cheater's brûlée, in that yogurt is used to cover a base of fruit, before being sprinkled with sugar and broiled.

Serves 4

INGREDIENTS

4 plums, pitted and sliced
2 cooking apples, peeled and sliced
1 teaspoon ground ginger
2$\frac{1}{2}$ cups plain yogurt, strained

2 tablespoons confectioners'
  sugar, sifted
1 teaspoon almond extract
$\frac{1}{3}$ cup raw brown crystal sugar

1 Put the plums and apples in a saucepan with 2 tablespoons of water and cook for 7–10 minutes, until tender but not mushy. Set aside to cool, then stir in the ginger.

2 Using a slotted spoon, spoon the mixture into the base of a shallow serving dish.

3 Mix together the strained plain yogurt, confectioners' sugar, and almond essence and spoon onto the fruit to cover it completely.

4 Sprinkle the raw brown crystal sugar over the top of the yogurt and cook under a preheated broiler for 3–4 minutes, or until the sugar has dissolved and formed a crust. Chill in the refrigerator for 1 hour and serve.

COOK'S TIP

Use any variety of fruit, such as mixed berries or mango pieces, for this dessert, but do not poach them.

VARIATION

You can vary the fruit in this dish, depending on what is in season—try fresh apricots or peaches. Alternatively, use a 14 ounce can of fruit cocktail.

Pear Cake

This is a really moist cake, flavored with chopped pears and cinnamon.

Serves 12

INGREDIENTS

4 pears, peeled and cored
vegetarian margarine, for greasing
2 tablespoons water
1½ cups all-purpose flour
2 teaspoons baking powder

½ cup light brown sugar
4 tablespoons milk
2 tablespoons honey, plus extra to drizzle
2 teaspoons ground cinnamon

2 egg whites

1 Grease and line the base of an 8-inch cake pan.

2 Put 1 pear in a food processor with the water and process until almost smooth. Transfer to a mixing bowl.

3 Sift in the all-purpose flour and baking powder. Beat in the sugar, milk, honey, and cinnamon and mix thoroughly with your fingers.

4 Chop all but one of the remaining pears and add to the mixture.

5 Whisk the egg whites until they form peaks and gently fold into the mixture until they are fully incorporated.

6 Slice the remaining pear and arrange in a fan pattern on the base of the pan.

7 Spoon the mixture into the pan and cook in a preheated oven at 300°F for 1¼–1½ hours, or until cooked through.

8 Remove the cake from the oven and let cool in the pan for 10 minutes.

9 Turn the cake out onto a wire cooling rack and drizzle with honey. Let cool completely, then cut into slices to serve.

COOK'S TIP

To test if the cake is cooked through, insert a toothpick into the center—if it comes out clean, the cake is cooked. If not, return the cake to the oven and test at frequent intervals.

Fruit & Nut Loaf

This loaf is like a fruit bread which may be served warm or cold,
perhaps spread with a little vegetarian margarine or butter or topped with jelly.

Makes 1 loaf

INGREDIENTS

1³/4 cups white cake flour, plus extra
  for dusting
¹/2 teaspoon salt
1 tablespoon vegetarian margarine,
  plus extra for greasing
2 tablespoons light brown sugar

²/3 cup golden raisins
¹/2 cup dried apricots, chopped
¹/2 cup chopped hazelnuts
2 teaspoons active dry yeast
6 tablespoons orange juice
6 tablespoons plain yogurt

2 tablespoons strained apricot
  conserve

1 Sift the flour and salt into a mixing bowl. Rub in the margarine and stir in the sugar, golden raisins, apricots, hazelnuts, and yeast.

2 Warm the orange juice in a saucepan, but do not allow it to boil.

3 Stir the warm orange juice into the flour mixture, together with the unsweetened yogurt, and bring the mixture together to form a dough.

4 Knead the dough on a lightly floured counter for 5 minutes until smooth and elastic. Shape into a round and place on a lightly greased cookie sheet. Cover with a clean dish cloth and leave to rise in a warm place until doubled in size.

5 Cook the loaf in a preheated oven at 425°F for about 35–40 minutes, until cooked through. Transfer to a cooling rack and brush with the apricot conserve. Let cool completely before serving.

COOK'S TIP

To test if the loaf is cooked
through—tap the base and if it
sounds hollow, it's cooked.

VARIATION

You can vary the nuts according
to whatever you have at hand—try
chopped walnuts or almonds.

Mixed Fruit Crumble

I have used tropical fruits in this crumble, flavored with ginger and coconut, for something a little different and very tasty.

Serves 4

INGREDIENTS

2 mangoes, sliced
1 papaya, seeded and sliced
8 ounces fresh pineapple, cubed
1 1/2 teaspoons ground ginger
8 tablespoons vegetarian margarine
1/2 cup light brown sugar

1 1/2 cups all-purpose flour
1/2 cup shredded coconut, plus extra
  to decorate

1 Place the fruit in a pan with 1/2 teaspoon of the ginger, 2 tablespoons of the margarine, and 1/4 cup of the sugar. Cook over gentle heat for 10 minutes, until the fruit softens. Spoon the fruit into the base of a shallow ovenproof dish.

2 Mix the flour and remaining ground ginger together. Rub in the remaining margarine with the fingertips until the mixture resembles fine bread crumbs. Stir in the remaining sugar and the coconut and spoon over the fruit to cover completely.

3 Cook the crumble in a preheated oven at 350°F for about 40 minutes, or until the top is crisp. Decorate with shredded coconut and serve.

VARIATION

Papayas have an orange-yellow skin and should yield to gentle pressure.

VARIATION

Use other fruits, such as plums, apples, or blackberries, as a fruit base and add chopped nuts to the topping instead of the coconut.

Fall Fruit Bread Pudding

*This is like a summer pudding, but it uses fruits which appear later in the year,
such as apples, pears, and blackberries, as a succulent filling.*

Serves 8

INGREDIENTS

4 cups mixed blackberries,
   chopped apples, chopped pears
³/₄ cup light brown sugar
1 teaspoon cinnamon

8 ounces white bread,
   thinly sliced, crusts removed
heavy cream, to serve (optional)

1 Place the fruit in a large saucepan with the light brown sugar, cinnamon, and 7 tablespoons of water, stir, and bring to a boil. Reduce the heat and simmer for 5–10 minutes so that the fruits soften, but still hold their shape.

2 Meanwhile, line the base and sides of a 4-cup bowl with the bread slices, ensuring that there are no gaps between the pieces of bread.

3 Spoon the fruit into the center of the bread-lined bowl and cover the fruit with the remaining bread.

4 Place a saucer on top of the bread and weight it down. Chill in the refrigerator overnight.

5 Turn the pudding out onto a serving plate and serve at once with cream, if desired.

COOK'S TIP

Stand the pudding on a plate when chilling to catch any juices that run down the sides of the bowl.

COOK'S TIP

This pudding would be delicious served with vegetarian vanilla ice cream to counteract the tartness of the blackberries.

Apple Fritters & Almond Sauce

These apple fritters are coated in a light, spiced batter
and deep-fried until crisp and golden. Serve warm.

Serves 4

INGREDIENTS

³/₄ cup all-purpose flour
pinch of salt
¹/₂ teaspoon ground cinnamon
³/₄ cup warm water
4 teaspoons vegetable oil
2 egg whites

2 eating apples, peeled
vegetable or sunflower oil, for
   deep-frying
cinnamon and sugar,
   to decorate

SAUCE:
1¹/₄ cups plain yogurt
¹/₂ teaspoon almond extract
2 teaspoons honey

1 Sift the flour and salt into a mixing bowl.

2 Add the cinnamon and mix well. Stir in the water and oil to make a smooth batter.

3 Whisk the egg whites until stiff peaks form and fold into the batter.

4 Using a sharp knife, cut the apples into chunks and dip the pieces of apple into the batter to coat.

5 Heat the oil for deep-frying to 350°F or until a cube of bread browns in 30 seconds. Fry the apple pieces, in batches, for 3–4 minutes, until golden brown and puffy.

6 Remove the apple fritters from the oil with a slotted spoon and drain on absorbent paper towels.

7 Mix together the superfine sugar and cinnamon and sprinkle it over the fritters.

8 Mix the sauce ingredients in a serving bowl and serve with the fritters.

VARIATION

Use pieces of banana or pineapple instead of the apple, if desired.

Cherry Crêpes

This dish can be made with either fresh pitted cherries or canned cherries for speed.

Serves 4

INGREDIENTS

FILLING:
14 ounce can pitted cherries,
   plus juice
$1/2$ teaspoon almond extract
$1/2$ teaspoon pumpkin pie spice
2 tablespoons cornstarch

CRÊPES:
$3/4$ cup all-purpose flour
pinch of salt
2 tablespoons chopped mint
1 egg
$1^1/4$ cups milk

vegetable oil, for frying
confectioners' sugar and toasted
   slivered almonds, to decorate

1 Put the cherries and $1^1/4$ cups of the juice in a pan with the almond extract and pumpkin pie spice. Stir in the cornstarch and bring to a boil, stirring until thickened and clear. Set aside until required.

2 To make the crêpes, sift together the flour and salt into a mixing bowl. Add the chopped mint and make a well in the center. Gradually beat in the egg and milk to make a smooth batter.

3 Heat 1 tablespoon of oil in a 7-inch skillet; pour off the oil when hot. Add just enough batter to coat the base of the skillet and cook for 1–2 minutes, or until the underside is cooked. Flip the crêpe over and cook for 1 minute. Remove from the skillet and keep warm. Heat 1 tablespoon of the oil in the skillet again and repeat to use up all the batter.

4 Spoon a quarter of the cherry filling onto a quarter of each pancake and fold the pancake into a cone shape. Dust with confectioners' sugar and sprinkle the slivered almonds over the top. Serve at once.

VARIATION

Use other fillings, such as gooseberries or blackberries, as an alternative to the cherries.

Lemon & Lime Syllabub

This dessert is rich, but absolutely delicious. It is not, however, for the calorie conscious as it contains a high proportion of cream, but it's well worth blowing the diet for!

Serves 4

INGREDIENTS

¹/₄ cup sugar
grated zest and juice of
  1 small lemon
grated zest and juice of
  1 small lime

4 tablespoons Marsala
  or medium sherry
1¹/₄ cups heavy cream
lime and lemon zest, to decorate

1 Put the sugar, fruit juices and zest and sherry in a bowl, mix well, and set aside to infuse for 2 hours.

2 Add the cream to the mixture and whisk until it just holds its shape.

3 Spoon the mixture into 4 tall serving glasses and chill in the refrigerator for 2 hours.

4 Decorate with lime and lemon zest and serve.

COOK'S TIP

Serve with almond cookies or uncoated florentines. Do not overwhip the cream when adding to the lemon and lime mixture, as it may curdle.

VARIATION

For an alternative citrus flavor, substitute two oranges for the lemon and lime, if desired.

COOK'S TIP

Replace the heavy cream with plain yogurt for a healthier version of this dessert, or use half quantities of both. Whisk the cream before adding to the yogurt.

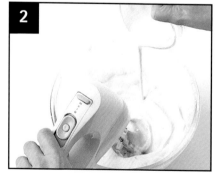

Banana & Mango Tart

Bananas and mangoes are a great combination of colors and flavors, especially when topped with toasted coconut chips.

Serves 8

INGREDIENTS

PASTRY:
8-inch baked pastry shell

FILLING:
2 small ripe bananas
1 mango, sliced
3^1/2 tablespoons cornstarch
6 tablespoons brown sugar
1^1/4 cups soy milk

^{2}/3 cup coconut milk
1 teaspoon vanilla extract
toasted coconut chips, to decorate

1 Slice the bananas and arrange half in the baked pastry shell with half of the mango pieces.

2 Put the cornstarch and sugar in a saucepan and mix together. Slowly stir in the soy and coconut milks until combined and cook over low heat, beating constantly, until the mixture thickens.

3 Stir in the vanilla extract, then pour the mixture over the fruit.

4 Top with the remaining fruit and toasted coconut chips. Chill in the refrigerator for 1 hour before serving.

COOK'S TIP

Coconut chips are available in some supermarkets and most health food shops. It is worth using them, as they look much more attractive and are not as sweet as shredded coconut.

COOK'S TIP

Choose mangoes with shiny and unblemished skins. To test whether they are ripe, gently cup the mango in your hand and squeeze gently— the mango should yield slightly to the touch.

Chocolate Tofu Cheesecake

This cheesecake takes a little time to prepare and cook but is well worth the effort. It is quite rich and is good served or decorated with a little fresh fruit, such as cherries or sliced strawberries.

Serves 12

INGREDIENTS

³/₄ cup all-purpose flour
³/₄ cup ground almonds
³/₄ cup raw brown crystal sugar
10 tablespoons vegetarian margarine
1¹/₂ pounds firm tofu
³/₄ cup vegetable oil
¹/₂ cup orange juice

³/₄ cup brandy
6 tablespoons unsweetened cocoa,
   plus extra to decorate
2 teaspoons almond extract
confectioners' sugar and Cape
   gooseberries, to decorate

1 Put the flour, ground almonds, and 1 tablespoon of the sugar in a bowl and mix well. Rub the margarine into the mixture with the fingertips to form a dough.

2 Lightly grease and line the base of a 9-inch springform pan. Press the dough into the base of the pan to cover, pushing the dough right up to the edge.

3 Roughly chop the tofu and put it in a food processor, together with all of the remaining ingredients, and process until smooth and creamy. Pour the purée over the base in the pan and cook in a preheated oven at 325°F for 1–1¼ hours, or until set.

4 Let cool in the pan for 5 minutes, then remove from the pan and chill in the refrigerator. Dust with confectioners' sugar and unsweetened cocoa. Decorate with cape gooseberries and serve.

COOK'S TIP

Cape gooseberries are of the same family as Chinese lanterns used in flower arrangements and have a sweet, sharp flavor.

Chocolate Fudge Pudding

This pudding has a hidden surprise when cooked, as it separates to give a rich chocolate sauce at the bottom of the dish.

Serves 4

INGREDIENTS

4 tablespoons vegetarian margarine, plus extra for greasing
6 tablespoons light brown sugar
2 eggs, beaten
1 1/4 cups milk
1/2 cup chopped walnuts

1/4 cup all-purpose flour
2 tablespoons unsweetened cocoa
confectioners' sugar and unsweetened cocoa, to dust

1 Lightly grease a 4-cup ovenproof dish.

2 Cream together the margarine and sugar in a large mixing bowl until fluffy. Beat in the eggs.

3 Gradually stir in the milk and add the walnuts.

4 Sift together the flour and unsweetened cocoa into the mixture and fold in gently, with a metal spoon, until well mixed.

5 Spoon the mixture into the prepared dish and cook in a preheated oven at 350°F for 35–40 minutes, or until the sponge is cooked and the top is firm to the touch.

6 Dust with confectioners' sugar and unsweetened cocoa.

COOK'S TIP

Serve this pudding with crème fraîche for a luxuriously rich dessert.

VARIATION

Add 1–2 tablespoons brandy or rum to the mixture for extra flavor, or 1–2 tablespoons orange juice for a child-friendly version.

Index

Index compiled by Lydia Darbyshire